STONEFLIES
FOR
THE ANGLER

ERIC LEISER
and
ROBERT H. BOYLE

DRAWINGS BY BILL ELLIOTT
PHOTOGRAPHS BY MATTHEW VINCIGUERRA

STONEFLIES FOR THE ANGLER

How to Know Them,
Tie Them, and
Fish Them

STACKPOLE
BOOKS

Acknowledgment for permission to use previously published material
as sources for drawings and tables is found on page 175.

Printed in the United States of America

10 9 8 7 6 5 4 3 2 1

This edition is reprinted by arrangement with Alfred A. Knopf, Inc.

Cover design by Tracy Patterson
Cover photographs by Norm Shires

Library of Congress Cataloging-in-Publication Data

Leiser, Eric, 1929–
    Stoneflies for the angler: how to know them, tie them, and fish
them/ Eric Leiser and Robert H. Boyle; drawings by Bill Elliott;
photographs by Matthew Vinciguerra.
      p.   cm.
    Includes bibliographical references
    ISBN 0-8117-2401-8
    1. Fly tying. 2. Stoneflies. 3. Fly fishing. I. Boyle, Robert
H. II. Title.
SH451.L433 1990
798.1'2—dc20
                                        90-9576
                                         CIP

CONTENTS

ILLUSTRATIONS   ix

PREFACE   xi

1. *A FLY FOR ALL SEASONS*   3

2. *STONEFLIES IN PERSPECTIVE*   9

3. *STONEFLY FAMILIES AND THEIR RELEVANCE TO ANGLING*   21

4. *IMITATING THE STONEFLY NYMPH*   43

5. *FISHING THE STONEFLY NYMPH*   77

6. *THE SECRET OF THE WHITE NYMPH*   99

7. *TYING AND FISHING THE STONEFLY ADULT*   107

8. *STONEFLY PATTERNS, NYMPHS AND ADULTS FOR ALL SEASONS, COAST TO COAST*   129

APPENDIX:
EMERGENCE TABLES   149

BIBLIOGRAPHY   159

INDEX   165

ILLUSTRATIONS

2-1   Behavioral drift patterns for a *Malenka* species, Right Fork, Logan River drainage, Utah, 1966   16

3-1   Glossa and paraglossa of a larval Euholognathe stonefly   22

3-2   Glossa and paraglossa of a larval Systellognathe stonefly   22

3-3   Nymphal wing pads   23

3-4   Tarsal segments of Euholognathe nymphs   25

3-5   *Taeniopteryx nivalis*   26

3-6   Nymphs of two species of perlid stoneflies   28

3-7   *Hesperoperla pacifica* adult   29

3-8   *Paragnetina media* nymph   31

3-9   *Hydroperla crosbyi* nymph   34

3-10   *Peltoperla* nymph   35

3-11   *Pteronarcys californica* nymph   37

3-12   *Allonarcys biloba* nymph   38

4-1   Weighting flat-bodied nymphs   46

4-2   Weighting oval-shaped nymphs   47

4-3   Weighting flat oval-shaped nymphs   48

4-4   Split shot added for weight   49

4-5   Flat, plastic underbody secured with thread   50

4-6   Preparing a quill sheathing strip   53

4-7   Preparing a wing case with the Renzetti wing burner   56

4-8 Tying the *Acroneuria*   60

4-9 Inverted *Acroneuria*   63

4-10 Tying Bill Simpson's *Acroneuria*   65

4-11 Tying the One-Feather Nymph   71

4-12 Black Woolly Worm   74

4-13 Black Woolly Bug   74

5-1 Mending line when casting across a stream or quartering upstream   81

5-2 Upstream hold cast   83

5-3 Monty Montplaisir's wet-fly technique   87

5-4 Ted Niemeyer's nymph-drifting technique   89

5-5 S curves for getting a nymph to the bottom   93

5-6 Casting while boat fishing   95

6-1 *Acroneuria* nymphs before and after molting   101

6-2 White Nymph   104

7-1 Tying the K's Butt Salmonfly   109

7-2 Tying the Salmonfly   118

7-3 *Pteronarcys californica* adult   123

Color plates of selected stonefly patterns follow page 82.

PREFACE

THIS BOOK IS FOR fly fishers. If others find it of use, wonderful. Among the flies that have long been of importance to trout and fishermen are the stoneflies—in fact, the oldest known artificial fly that has retained its original name is the large wet "Stone Fly" described in *The Treatise of Fishing with an Angle* written in England some five hundred years ago. Yet very little has been written about these flies from the angler's point of view. In this book, it is our intention to do not only that but to simplify what otherwise might strike the reader as a complex order of insects.

To accomplish this, we have fished, collected specimens, tied flies—nymphs, wet and dry flies—tested them, and consulted with other fly fishers and tyers. Among the most notable of our colleagues have been R. "Monty" Montplaisir of Colebrook, New Hampshire, Jay Neve of Bellevue, Michigan, Don Fox of Chassel, Michigan, Gary Borger of Wausau, Wisconsin, Charles E. Brooks and Craig Mathews of West Yellowstone, Montana, Dave McNeese of Salem, Oregon, Paul Schmookler of the Bronx, New York, and Dr. Wilbur G. Downs of Branford, Connecticut.

We have also ransacked the scientific literature and talked at length with specialists in the order Plecoptera—the stoneflies—most notably Dr. Kenneth W. Stewart of North Texas State University, who gladly put up with our barrage of questions and sent us away laden with papers and specimens. Other scientists whose help we would like to acknowledge include Rebecca F. Surdick of College Park, Maryland, Dr. Sandy B. Fiance of Dobbs Ferry, New York, Dr. Dominick J. Pirone of Manhattan College, Dr. Stephen W. Hitchcock of the Connecticut Department of Environmental Protection, Dr. Thomas F. Waters of the University of Minnesota, Dr. Norman H. Anderson of Oregon State University, Dr. Richard W. Baumann of Brigham Young University, Dr. Richard J. Neves of the Virginia Cooperative Fishery Research Unit at Virginia Polytechnic Institute and State University, Dr. H. B. N. Hynes of the University of Waterloo in Ontario, Dr. P. P. Harper of the University of Montreal, Mr. Stanley G. Jewett, Jr., of West Linn, Oregon, Dr. William E. Ricker of Nanaimo, British Columbia, and Dr. James Atz of the American Museum of Natural History, in New York City, whose generosity never flags.

Any mistakes are ours, and animal behavior, be it of stoneflies or trout, is not a hundred percent predictable. In following our advice, you're going to run into stoneflies and trout that didn't read this book. But we do think that you're going to run into a lot of trout that might say, "By God, this character not only read the book, but he memorized page 97."

Finally, we would like to thank our agent, John Cushman, and our editor, Angus Cameron of Knopf, who did memorize every page, and Barbara Bristol and John Woodside who saw to it that they came out in order.

—Eric Leiser
Robert H. Boyle

STONEFLIES
FOR
THE ANGLER

1

A FLY FOR
ALL SEASONS

One may say that trout and stoneflies are intimately
associated; where one occurs, the other also is found.

—Richard A. Muttkowski, "The Ecology of Trout
Streams in Yellowstone National Park"

FOR YEARS YOU'VE HEARD ABOUT the salmonfly hatch in Montana. Now the
word is out—"The hatch is on!"—and you're on your way, another member of an army of anglers composed of Buena Vista orthodontists,
Wall Street brokers, working stiffs from Toledo, Memphis
accountants, Philadelphia lawyers, and Boston
Brahmins who go by way of Dedham.
After a restless night in the motel in West Yellowstone, you're
at last on the banks of the Madison. The scene is everything
you've been led to believe and then some. The salmonflies,
Pteronarcys californica—plump juicy insects 2 inches long with great
gauzy wings—are everywhere. Their nymphal shucks litter the rocks
on shore. Adults hang like clusters of grapes in the willows reaching
over the bank, and when not making love in the bushes, where in sheer

buggy ecstasy they sometimes tumble off the couch into the maws of a Peeping Tom trout, they fly awkwardly above the river by the thousands. Females dapple the water surface to shed their eggs, and the trout are waiting for them. Caught by a gust of wind, other salmonflies are dashed to the water. These lumbering flies appear to have no sense of fear or self-preservation. They even land on your hat and shoulders.

Brushing them aside and atremble with bug fever, you assemble your rod, put on the reel, strip line through the guides, and tie on a Sofa Pillow, a Bird's Stonefly, or—best of all—the K's Butt described in chapter 7. As you start your cast, you stumble on the rocks, the line wraps around you, and the fly lands only a foot from shore. As you slap your pockets to find your glasses, the line suddenly goes taut. Forget the glasses, raise the tip. With aplomb, you manage to land a 12-inch brown. A nice fish back home, but nothing here, and with a laugh at your own luck, you return the trout to the river. These fish must be crazy, you think to yourself.

Indeed they are, as you discover with your second cast, this one 35 feet out in front of a rock. The fly dances briefly in the current, and then there is a savage strike. This fish is a 16-incher. Fish are rising all over the river. The 15-incher you get on the fourth cast has salmonflies stuffed in its gullet. The trout can't seem to get enough; they're in a frenzy like bluefish chopping up bunkers in Long Island Sound. The trout have abandoned all caution. Two hours later, the action stops; the gorged fish have had their fill for the day.

So goes the salmonfly hatch, which can last for weeks as it moves upstream. To see the salmonfly hatch is to witness one of the great prodigalities of nature. And it happens in much of the West. It happens on other rivers in Montana, Wyoming, Colorado, California, Oregon, Idaho, and Washington. Millions of salmonflies? There must be billions. And the fish know it.

It's the last day of your trip, you've got less than an hour to fish before you have to return the rental car at the airport, and a cold rain has put down the hatch. A friend at the motel suggests you try a nymph. A couple of days before emerging, the nymphs move toward shore before clambering out to split their skins and join the swinging party in the bushes. On the river, the nymph doesn't get any takes on your first few casts; it's traveling too high and too fast in the current. Time is fleeting, and you quickly press a split shot on the leader and cast again. As the nymph swings in the current, a fish takes. A 12-incher that you release. Another cast. A blank. Another cast, and there's a take that makes you feel as though you've grabbed the other end of the universe. But then the fish breaks off. Your hands are shaking as you pack up to leave. You'll always wonder about that fish. Six pounds? Eight? Twelve? But what you do know for sure is that it really walloped the big nymph, and maybe you ought to try it back home.

Just such a thought occurred to Matt Vinciguerra, the photographer and fly-tyer, who, after fishing in Montana, returned home to Brewster, New York, where he tied up a big Western-style nymph with some raw brown wool he had bought at Bob Jacklin's in West Yellowstone. Matt knew that the nymphs of *Pteronarcys dorsata* and *Allonarcys biloba,* found in the East and Middle West, very closely resemble their Western cousin. In mid-November, Matt drove up to the Catskills to see a friend and, in the course of the visit, he learned that the Esopus was still open to fishing. Matt borrowed a rod, drove to the stream, and cast the nymph in a run. Bango, a 23-inch rainbow. Pressed for time, Matt had to return home, but he came back a week later with the nymph and took two more rainbows, one 21 inches, the other 19 inches. "Eastern fishermen usually don't fish big stonefly nymphs," says Matt, whose nymph is described in chapter 8. "They think big nymphs are for out West, but we have big nymphs, and they obviously take big fish."

One of these big stoneflies, *P. dorsata,* is actually transcontinental in range. It occurs from Labrador south to Florida—and whoever thought of Florida as stonefly country?—and extends westward to Wyoming. It has even been found in Alaska, a state with a curious stonefly population. Alaska has next to nothing in the way of big golden stones, the Perlidae, and really very few *P. dorsata,* but many rivers harbor an abundance of *P. dorsata*'s smaller second cousin, *Pteronarcella badia,* which is a look-alike except that the nymph reaches only an inch in length at maturity.

Fly fishermen who haven't fished stoneflies, or who have fished them only casually, don't realize what opportunities imitations of these insects offer to anglers. As Matt Vinciguerra demonstrated, you don't have to go to Montana to score. To be sure, the Montana hatches can't be beat, but there's a chance your best fish might be had in your own backyard with a stonefly. Along with mayflies and caddis, stoneflies are a staple of the trout diet, but when it comes to offering a big fish its choice of fare, all other things being equal, it will opt for the medium to large stonefly nymph. Stonefly patterns, nymph, wet, or dry, can also be effective on smallmouth bass and Atlantic salmon. In fact, we have taken striped bass, a species that can be very choosy, on stonefly nymph imitations in the lower Croton River, a tidal tributary of the Hudson that is bereft of stoneflies.

Stoneflies belong to the order Plecoptera, the Greek for "plaited wings," because of the way in which the typical adult folds its four wings flat over the abdomen when at rest. As aquatic insects, stoneflies were all but designed for the fly fisherman. They can be found almost anywhere in a stream, depending on the habitat preference of a species. Although some live up to the name stonefly by living under rocks and stones, many might be called "debrisflies" because they inhabit submerged masses of twigs and leaves or the rotting limbs of trees that have fallen into the water.

Some species are active during the day, while others are nocturnal. The emergence dates for different stonefly species are spread over the course of the year. Little *Allocapnia* and some other species emerge in the winter. The adults of these so-called "winter stoneflies" can often be seen trotting about on the snow adjacent to a stream. On streams that are open to winter fishing, imitations of either the nymph or adult can be lethal.

Any fisherman who starts delving into stoneflies will find them fascinating, not only as insects to imitate in order to catch fish, but as animals in their own right. If you ever start turning over rocks in a stream or paw your way through leaf litter, as we have for years, you'll soon realize that some insects are more interesting than others. Cranefly larvae, big pulpy blobs, are a bore. So are many mayfly nymphs, although *Isonychia* is a crowd pleaser that comes on like Speedy Alka-Seltzer. But most stoneflies have a certain something about them. There is tiny *Peltoperla*, which looks like a miniature armored cockroach; rapacious *Acroneuria*, which will try to bite your finger; and the docile *Pteronarcys* and *Allonarcys*, which will curl up in your hand.

We're not alone in our pro-Plecoptera feelings. Some people can really become smitten with stoneflies. The prize case is Paul Schmookler, who runs 20th Century Angler, Ltd., and sells Insecta Slides—individually identified specimens of mayflies, caddis, stoneflies, and other aquatic insects embedded in clear polyacrylic blocks. Paul is fond of just about every insect—at present he's trying to talk the editors of *Fly Fisherman* into doing a centerfold on a different one in each issue—but he loves stoneflies the most. He ties incredibly realistic *Acroneuria* nymphs, using a photocopying process (see Plate 3), and he is planning to design a nymphal suit (complete with antennae, tails, and gill tufts which would sprout from his chest) that he can wear lolling around his Bronx apartment or to a costume ball. He is also thinking of taking a swim in it in the Delaware to see how the trout react.

Before the last presidential primaries in New York, Paul was at home one evening in his apartment, a Peter Lorre smile playing over his face while he looked over his collection of stoneflies entombed in their transparent mausoleums, when the phone rang. It was a woman taking a political survey.

"Are you a Republican?" she asked.

"No," said Schmookler just before the line went click, "I'm a Plecopteran."

2

STONEFLIES
IN PERSPECTIVE

THE ORDER PLECOPTERA IS SMALL, with approximately 1,500 species of stoneflies known worldwide. At last count, 510 of these species lived in the United States and Canada. But don't let those numbers boggle your mind; 510 species is less than the total number of either mayfly or caddis species, and there's no way anyhow that you're going to have to tie 510 different nymphs or 510 different adults. For one thing, some stonefly species are of no real consequence to you as a fisherman. Then again, so many species look so much alike that an expert entomologist can have (and often does have) difficulty identifying them. A relative handful of patterns—nymph, wet fly, and dry fly—will serve you hand-somely. As a friend of ours, Dr. Kenneth W. Stewart of North Texas State University, says, "If I have to use a microscope to tell the difference between species, it can't make any difference to the trout." Ken Stewart knows what he's talking about. He and Bill Stark at Mississippi College are in the fourth year of a five-year grant from the National Science Foundation to do the definitive study of the stonefly nymphs of North America.

A stonefly passes through three stages in the course of its life. There is the egg, which hatches underwater; the nymph, which lives under-water; and the terrestrial adult, a clumsy flier that can often be seen resting on bushes, stones, or bridges near the streambank. Depending on species, the life cycle of a stonefly lasts from one to three years, with the majority of time spent in the nymphal stage.

To grow, the nymphs must shed their external skins by molting. Stonefly nymphs generally undergo from 10 to 20 molts in the course of development, and the stage between molts is known as an instar. During the molting period itself, the nymph becomes colorless, a creamy white, for several hours, a phenomenon we deal with at length in chapter 6 because of its potential importance to the nymph fisherman.

Stonefly nymphs may be readily separated from those of mayflies by their two claws rather than one on each leg, by their lack of gills on the middle abdominal segments, and by their two segmented tails or cerci. Mayflies usually have three cerci, always a single claw on each leg, and gills in variable locations on the middle abdomen.

Adult stoneflies emerge after the mature nymphs crawl from the stream onto the bank or onto logs, branches, or stones above the water. Males emerge first in many species, and are about two-thirds the size of the females. In searching for females, the males of some species send out drumming signals by beating their abdomens on the ground, and the drumming signals for each species are very specific. For instance, the male of *Pteronarcys dorsata* gives five hard knocks with his abdomen, and a virgin female of the species that picks up the vibrations will answer with six softer knocks. The signaling continues until the male finds the female with the right vibes. Mated females do not drum. Ken Stewart, who has recorded the signals of a number of species, has actually gotten some females to respond by playing a tape recording of the male. "When I want to get going in the morning, I'll play a tape of drumming signals," Stewart says. "I think it's just tremendous. Every trout fisherman should have a tape of stonefly signals to shore him up through fishing lulls."

To oviposit, females fly or walk about, dipping their abdomens in the water. Some females drop their egg mass into the water, but with most species the female usually floats on the surface and the egg mass washes off before she flies away. In the water, the individual eggs separate and sink to the bottom. The eggs of some species have a sticky outer coating that adheres to the bottom, while other eggs, such as those of *Perlesta placida,* have numerous filaments with flared tips that hold fast in crevices. In the ordinary course of events, the eggs hatch within a few weeks to start the life cycle anew, although the eggs and nymphs of some species can go into "diapause," a state of arrested development, for months.

The nymphs of stoneflies generally live in cool, well-oxygenated streams, although a few species are found in the northern United States and Canada in deep, cold lakes, with rocky, windswept shores. In fact, one species, *Capnia lacustra,* spends its adult stage in the depths of Lake Tahoe. There are some other species, such as *Paraperla* and *Isocapnia,* that spend their nymphal stage living in rock and gravel rubble at least a dozen feet underground, beneath the bottoms of rivers, such as the Tobacco and the Flathead in Montana. These nymphs are often pale in color, like a nymph in perpetual molt, and they surface from their subterranean habitat only to emerge as adults.

A water temperature of 77 degrees Fahrenheit is about the maximum nymphs of most species can withstand. Few species can take warm water, poor oxygenation, siltation, or pollution, all of which have eliminated stoneflies in many of their former habitats. Today, no one associates stoneflies with major polluted rivers in this country, but a hundred and fifty years ago Thomas Say, the pioneer American entomologist, found *Pteronarcys dorsata* numerous in May near Pittsburgh on the Ohio River, while *Paragnetina immarginata,* wrote Say, "appears in considerable numbers towards the end of May." Even many rural areas have lost their stoneflies. Dr. William L. Hilsenhoff of the University of Wisconsin reports that "low levels of pollution from pasturing cattle probably account for their absence from most streams in agricultural areas of southeastern Wisconsin." But although many fishermen look upon stoneflies as biological indicators of clean water, Ken Stewart cautions that "there is considerable variation in sensitivity to pollutants between species. We need to correlate stonefly species with their oxygen and temperature tolerances, and their sensitivity to various other chemical and physical conditions. Although this will require a tremendous research effort, it would give us an enhanced ability to predict the health of a stream by the nature of its stonefly fauna."

Until a decade or so ago, stonefly research proceeded at a rather slow pace in this country. For one thing, researchers had to expend considerable effort collecting and classifying species. For another, not many entomologists specialized in the order Plecoptera. There wasn't any money in it, and then again, the order has a very small number of species, especially when compared with beetles or butterflies and moths, with their tens of thousands of members (there are 280,000 known species of beetles in the world; in fact, there are more species of beetles than of plants and trees). Even beyond this, research on the Plecoptera was set back by the untimely deaths of Dr. Peter W. Claassen of Cornell in 1937 and Dr. Theodore H. Frison of the Illinois Natural History Survey in 1945. "The death of its two foremost students, both in the prime of life, was and remains a serious setback to stonefly study in North America," William E. Ricker, an outstanding student of stoneflies in his own right, wrote in 1952. Still, stoneflies have attracted some remarkable minds. Ricker himself is one. He is one of the greatest biologists in the world. Besides his work in stonefly systematics, he is the premier authority in the world on fish population dynamics and is the father of modern fishery science.

In good part, the start of the environmental movement in the late 1960s prompted the current resurgence of interest in stoneflies and other aquatic insects. In 1973, the Entomological Society of America formally created its Aquatic Insects Subsection in recognition of the new interest, and in 1974 the Midwest Benthological Society, which had been founded in 1953 with 13 charter members, changed its name to the North American Benthological Society (NABS) to reflect its expanding national and international membership. NABS, which has a stonefly nymph as its emblem, now has over 1,100 members. Only last year a Dutch publishing company launched a new quarterly journal, *Aquatic Insects,* edited by Dr. Joachim Illies, a West German stonefly specialist.

Every few years, stonefly specialists throughout the world get together to read papers and compare notes. The Sixth International Symposium on Plecoptera was held in Schlitz, West Germany, in 1977, and the Seventh in Nara, Japan, in August 1980. Between meetings, the specialists, or Plecopterists as they call themselves, can keep in touch with one another through *Perla,* a newsletter edited by Dr. Richard W. Baumann at Brigham Young University and Dr. Peter Zwick of the Max Planck Institute for Limnology in Schlitz, West Germany. The idea of *Perla* was hatched at the Fourth International Symposium on Plecoptera, held in Abisko, in Swedish Lapland, in 1968, but the first issue did not appear until 1974. "It might appear to be late to outsiders," Baumann wrote, "but anyone familiar with the habits of many stoneflies should not be surprised. . . . Even after oviposition, development is often not straightforward and considerable spans of time may be spent in the dormant stages."

Much of the present research on the order Plecoptera deals with aspects of stonefly behavior and ecology, such as food. Although a number of stonefly nymphs are carnivores, most are detritovores, feeding not on the submerged vegetation within a stream itself but on allochthonous debris, derived from plant material that has fallen, blown, or washed into the stream. If you have ever wondered about what happens to the dead leaves that wind up in a stream, we'll give you the answer: Many stoneflies chomp on them, and you can see this if you reach down into the stream and pick up a handful of dead leaves that have been "skeletonized." The fleshy part of the blades will have been chewed to bits, while the tougher midrib and veins, like the bones in a roast beef, will still be intact. But note this: Some stoneflies apparently eat the leaves only when the surfaces have been colonized by microorganisms, mainly fungi and bacteria. In other words, these stoneflies will only eat their roast beef after it has been seasoned, or their bread after "peanut butter" has been added.

But there is even more to this. Research indicates that some species of stoneflies eat only certain kinds of leaves. For example, in stream cages set up by Dr. Stephen W. Hitchcock, *Peltoperla maria* "skeletonized dead leaves of maple and beech but fed only sparingly on oak." Given the correct association of nymphs with specific leaves, the day may come, crazy as it sounds, when the knowledgeable angler will know what pattern to use on a strange stream simply by identifying the trees along the banks. Conversely, you might wonder about which stoneflies are no longer to be found in a stream because of logging practices, highway construction, or other effects on the trees of a watershed. The toll must be considerable. In an interesting experiment, E. F. Benfield, D. S. Jones, and M. F. Patterson placed packets of American sycamore leaves in purselike baskets in the North Fork of the Roanoke River in Virginia. The American sycamore is the dominant riparian tree on the North Fork, which flows through pastureland. Retrieving the baskets for study, Benfield and his colleagues found no *Pteronarcys,* even though those large stoneflies abound in tributaries of the North Fork of the Roanoke. They hypothesized that the absence of *Pteronarcys* was caused by the practice of clearcutting the valley floor to provide pasture, which left "a riparian vegetation of limited composition." As Dr. H. B. N. Hynes notes in his "Biology of Plecoptera," stoneflies are "adversely affected by almost every kind of activity of technological man."

In the natural state, detritovorous stoneflies are an important link in the energy flow that goes from the sun, soil, and trees to dead leaves to stoneflies to trout—and man. A burgeoning scientific literature now exists on this very subject. N. K. Kaushik and Hynes have written on "The Fate of the Dead Leaves That Fall Into Streams," and W. F. McDiffett, who studied the stonefly *Pteronarcys scotti*—now known as *Allonarcys scotti* — in a north Georgia trout stream, calculated that a single nymph consumed so many leaves that it produced more than 15 percent of its body weight per day in fecal material. On the West Coast, D. W. Chapman figured out that more than half the energy used by young Coho salmon in Oregon coastal streams originated as dead leaves or other organic matter that came from the land. In sum, it is impossible to overemphasize the importance of dead leaves to stream ecosystems. As Dr. Dominick J. Pirone of Manhattan College, who is an entomologist, ardent fisherman, and the finest all-round field naturalist we have ever known, puts it: "To most people, it's a pain when leaves fall. Yet one of the biggest transfers of energy on this planet is the leaf fall."

Another important aspect of some stoneflies and other stream invertebrates is what is now known as "behavioral drift." Back in the summer of 1927, Dr. Paul R. Needham set out to collect terrestrial insects that fell onto the surfaces of trout streams in central New York. To do so, he stretched a fine-meshed net across the streams for one-hour sampling periods during the daytime. More than 93 percent of the catch was composed of adult insects terrestrial in origin, but the rest of the catch consisted of aquatic nymphs, larvae, and pupae which, Needham thought, "happened to be washed from their hiding places and swept downstream." In the years that followed, others investigated and concluded that the continuous drift of invertebrates was a natural feature of streams. But there was much more to it than that, as evidenced by the research of Hikaru Tanaka, a Japanese scientist.

In 1960 Tanaka published a paper with a very long but very important title, "On the Daily Change of the Drifting of Benthic Animals in Stream, Especially on the Types of Daily Change Observed in Taxonomic Groups of Insects." By the types of daily change, Tanaka was referring to the "diel periodicity," the response by organisms to the 24-hour light/dark cycle of each day, and what he found was that the amount of drift by bottom insects increases greatly at night, particularly in the hours following sunset.

After Tanaka's revelation, Dr. Thomas F. Waters of the University of Minnesota, who had discovered nocturnal behavioral drift himself in

1959, and Karl Müller in Sweden followed with papers in the early 1960s. These papers by Müller, Waters, and Tanaka stimulated research by other investigators, and as a result, the literature on behavioral drift has been accumulating at an exponential rate.

Here are some of the key findings thus far:

Behavioral drift mainly occurs at night, and it is triggered by decreasing light intensity. For many species, sunset is almost like flicking a switch. Decreasing light intensity, Waters wrote in a 1972 review, "apparently acts in an 'on-off' fashion, triggering the insects' increased activity as it falls to some threshold level of intensity, which appears to be about 1 to 5 lux (0.1 to 0.5 foot-candles) measured at the water surface. . . . There also appear to be differences among species in response and threshold level." In other words, different floats for different folks.

There are usually two peaks in nighttime behavioral drift. For most aquatic insects, the major peak occurs in the first few hours after darkness. The drift then decreases during the night and peaks again (in a minor fashion) just before dawn. This is called the "bigeminus" pattern of behavioral drift. The opposite is the "alternans" pattern. Here the minor peak takes place after sunset while the major peak occurs before dawn. Most stoneflies follow the bigeminus pattern. The nymphs can determine light intensity through their ocelli, the little simple eyes on the dorsal surfaces of their heads.

Figure 2–1 shows the behavioral drift patterns for stonefly nymphs of a *Malenka* species, collected by T. F. Waters in 1966 from Right Fork, Logan River drainage, in northeast Utah. The dark circle marks sunset and the light circle dawn.

The patterns shown in Figure 2–1 appear to be of the bigeminus type. Waters notes that "this species has its propensity to drift in early life history stages. The nymphs in August were approaching maturity."

More behavioral drift occurs on dark nights than on moonlit nights. Dr. Norman H. Anderson of Oregon State University lit up a stream at night, and the lighting reduced the amount of drift to the daytime level. "Several investigators have varied light experimentally," Waters wrote, "using artificial light during the normal night and darkening during the daytime, with essentially similar results: drift virtually ceased with the application of light and increased when darkness was experimentally applied during the day. Some authors report continued periodicities for some time, at least for several species, in continuous darkening produced experimentally." Continuous light, however, "eliminates a drift

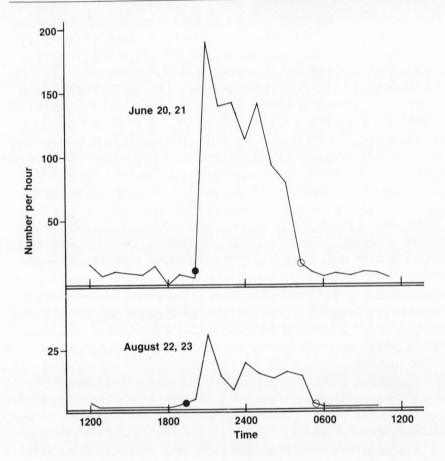

Figure 2–1. Behavioral drift patterns for a *Malenka* species, Right Fork, Logan River drainage, Utah, 1966.

periodicity, either artificially or in the natural light of the polar summer or even possibly in moonlight."

According to Waters, the stream insects that are "most important quantitatively in drift" are the Ephemeroptera, the family Simuliidae of the Diptera, the Trichoptera, and the Plecoptera, apparently in that order. "Additionally," Waters noted, "amphipods of the genus *Gammarus* are frequently reported in marked periodicities and high drift rates, especially in calcareous streams; the isopod, *Asellus*, has also been observed to drift in a diel periodicity. In most of these groups, there are species exhibiting no apparent behavioral drift, even though sometimes abundant in the bottom fauna. On the other hand, the mayfly genus *Baetis* appears universally to exhibit high drift rates and marked periodicities."

Thomas J. Cloud, Jr., and Ken Stewart, who studied the drift of mayflies in the Brazos River, found that without exception, *all* of the Brazos River mayfly nymphs drifted at night. Moreover, they wrote, "In each species, highest drift densities were generally recorded immediately following sunset." Cloud and Stewart could almost set their watches by the *Baetis* species. In the month of June, the maximum drift density for *Baetis* occurred at 1.5 hours after sunset. Cloud and Stewart also found that while the Brazos River mayflies drifted at night throughout the year, "All Mayfly populations studied exhibited their greatest drift densities during the summer sample months of June and August. This is not unlike the findings of previous authors who have found basically the same pattern of seasonal invertebrate drift in other regional, stream ecosystems."

During the twelve 5-hour sampling times in June, Cloud and Stewart estimated that 5.63×10^4 *Baetis* drifted past their sample transect. That's 56,000 nymphs. But that doesn't even begin to compare with the numbers of *Baetis* reported in 1968 by W. D. Pearson and D. R. Franklin on the Green River in Wyoming. In one 24-hour period, an estimated 170×10^6 *Baetis* nymphs drifted past their sampling station. That's 170 million nymphs, the greatest estimate of total drift for any species of invertebrate.

Drifting nymphs are everywhere in the water column, from top to bottom. How far do they drift? *Gammarus* has drifted 130 meters in a night, *Baetis* about 100. Nymphs of the stonefly *Calineuria californica,* formerly classified within the genus *Acroneuria,* have drifted, in the course of a year, from more than a 2,000-foot altitude in a stream to 200 feet above sea level. Just why do so many aquatic insects drift? Ken Stewart says that "drift is thought to be a population relief valve, and certain insects, such as stoneflies, that have a high reproductive capacity launch themselves into the water column, drift downstream and test their environment. They can sense crowding and competition for food. Carnivorous stoneflies are highly territorial, and they stake out their territory in a limited amount of substrate. Let another nymph come near, and the challenged nymph will whip its tail around." Stewart says he has no "problem with the idea that an insect can adapt to launching itself into the current with reducing light intensity. If a wasp can dig a hole in the ground, go off, get prey and bring it back a half mile to the hole, I can see where an insect will use drift to move to new territory."

What does all this mean to the fish? According to Waters, "Salmonids, particularly, select and defend territories that are the best suited for the interception of drift; the size and location of the territory is determined by the drift density and patterns of drift in the water currents." In the Pyrenees, J. M. Elliott studied the food of brown and rainbow trout in a mountain stream in relation to the abundance of drifting invertebrates. He found that the food of the trout was similar in percentage composition to that of the drift, and that there was a good correlation between the daily changes in the amount of food in the stomachs of the fish and changes in the abundance of drifting invertebrates. Moreover, Elliott noted, "The major feeding period was in the early hours of the night when the trout fed chiefly on benthic invertebrates in the drift."

In Idaho, J. S. Griffith, Jr., studied the utilization of invertebrate drift by brook and cutthroat trout in four small streams. He found that members of five insect orders, Ephemeroptera, Coleoptera, Diptera, Trichoptera, and Plecoptera, composed 97 percent of the number of drifting invertebrates, and an average of 92 percent of the number of organisms eaten by the brook and cutthroat trout. Most mayflies, stoneflies, and aquatic beetles drifted at night; the terrestrial component of both drift and diet was "insignificant."

Recently, J. David Allan studied trout predation and drift in Cement Creek, a Colorado trout stream. The mayfly *Baetis bicaudatus* in the creek has two generations in a single year, so at certain times there are two groups or "cohorts" of *B. bicaudatus* in the stream, with the members of the older cohort larger in size. Allan examined the stomachs of a series of brook trout collected in July, August, and September. He collected the trout at least 3 to 4 hours after dawn or dusk in order to reduce the possibility that food in the stomachs of the fish had come from feeding during the daylight hours. Here is what Allan discovered:

The trout collected on July 7 and 8 had fed heavily on the larger *B. bicaudatus* nymphs. The trout collected on August 8 and 9 ate a few *B. bicaudatus* nymphs. The larger nymphs had already emerged, and only the smaller ones were available. The trout collected on September 8 and 9 also ate only a few *B. bicaudatus* nymphs. Instead the trout had switched to feeding on the nymphs of the stonefly *Zapada haysi,* a nemourid, that "exceeded *B. bicaudatus* in body size by September and became the preferred prey."

Allan noted that trout feeding at night not only avoided the smallest prey but "positively selected" the largest prey. He added, "Selection for larger prey by fish feeding on invertebrates has been documented extensively. Studies of rainbow trout *(Salmo gairdneri)* have demonstrated that reaction distance increases with prey size . . . and that larger insects in the surface drift are taken in preference to smaller insects. . . . My study extends this pattern to brook trout *(S. fontinalis)* feeding on drifting insect nymphs."

3

STONEFLY FAMILIES AND THEIR RELEVANCE TO ANGLING

STONEFLIES IN NORTH AMERICA ARE DIVIDED into two groups—the Euh_lognatha and the Systellognatha—on the basis of their mouthparts. The names refer to the jaws of the insects; Euholognatha is the Greek word for "normal jaws," and Figure 3–1 shows why. The mouthparts known as the glossae and paraglossae, representative of this group, extend about the same distance. By contrast, Systellognatha is the Greek word for "contracted jaws." In this group, except for the Peltoperlidae and the Pteronarcyidae, the glossae are set further back than the paraglossae (Figure 3–2).

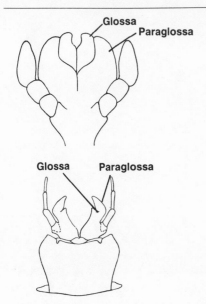

Figure 3–1. Glossa and paraglossa of a larval Euholognathe stonefly, *Taeniopteryx nivalis*. Note that these jaw parts extend about the same distance.

Figure 3–2. Glossa and paraglossa of a larval Systellognathe stonefly, *Isogenus subvarians*. Note that the glossae are set further back than the paraglossae.

There are four families in the Euholognatha and five in the Systellognatha. The Euholognatha have several features in common besides their mouthparts: almost all of the nymphs in this group eat detritus, the insects are usually small in size at maturity, and are brown to black in color.

EUHOLOGNATHA

The Leuctridae

This family has 40 species, usually brown to black in color. The wing pads of the nymph are parallel to the body axis (Figure 3–3), and the wings of the adults tend to curl laterally around the abdomen when at rest. The wings are dark. *Paraleuctra occidentalis* is a common species in the West, with adults emerging from February to August.

Unfortunately, very little is known about the life histories and behavior of the Leuctridae except for two species, *Zealeuctra claasseni* and *Z. hitei*. Since the latter is confined to Texas, we can forget about it as far as trout fishing goes; however, *Z. claasseni* also occurs in West Virginia and the Ozarks, so we'll report on what Rosalyn K. Snellen and Ken

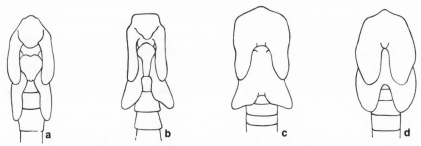

Figure 3–3. Nymphal wing pads. *(a)* Leuctridae. *(b)* Capniidae. *(c)* Perlodidae. *(d)* Chloroperlidae.

Stewart found when they studied that species in Texas; their findings might prove of angling value.

The *Z. claasseni* nymphs, which are dark brown in color, live in gravel and rock rubble riffles, and apparently feed on the dead leaves of black willow, sycamore, and several species of oak and elm. In Texas, they emerge from late October through February, during the day. The adults are also active during the day. The females walk or fly along the water surface to deposit their egg mass, with oviposition taking place during the early morning, late afternoon, and evening.

The Capniidae

There are 129 species in this family, but don't panic. The nymphs are small—most less than 12 millimeters—and dark brown, and one pattern could serve for all. The male adult of *Allocapnia maria,* a March emerger, is the smallest Northeastern stonefly, measuring only 3 millimeters long from the head to the end of the wings. The tails of Capniidae generally range from at least half as long to as long as the body. M. J. Coleman and H. B. N. Hynes, who studied the bottom fauna of a southern Ontario stream, the Speed River, which was frozen over from mid-December to mid-April, reported that mature nymphs of *Allocapnia pygmaea* "occurred from mid-February" and that "a few specimens emerged in March through small holes in the ice. The ice began to break up on 15 April 1966, and thousands of adults emerged on that day, by crawling up onto the ice blocks."

The Capniidae, some Leuctridae, and the Taeniopterygidae are the three families that mainly constitute the so-called winter stoneflies. "The winter stoneflies belong to a physiologically peculiar group of organisms,"

Herbert H. Ross and William E. Ricker wrote in *The Classification, Evolution and Dispersal of the Winter Stonefly Genus,* ALLOCAPNIA. "With the approach of winter, many living things are normally thought of as becoming quiescent or dormant. In the temperate regions, leaves fall from the trees, the crops are harvested, the sound of crickets declines, and flowers with their attendant multitude of insects disappear from the landscape. For a few insects, however, winter heralds not a cessation but an acceleration of activity. . . . Among the most abundant of the active winter insects in temperate North America are the winter stoneflies."

Winter stoneflies did much to stimulate interest in the order Plecoptera. During the 1920s Theodore H. Frison and another entomologist at the Illinois Natural History Survey liked to hike in the hilly country near Urbana. They noticed that in some of the smaller brooks feeding into the Salt Fork River, the size of the smallest stonefly nymphs kept increasing as winter approached. Intrigued by this, Frison began to study the nymphs, about which almost nothing was known, and they turned out to be winter stoneflies. Frison then went on to study other stonefly families, not only in Illinois, but all across North America, setting the stage for the modern classification of this order.

The Nemouridae

There are 61 species in the family Nemouridae, and the giveaway for the dull to dark brown small nymphs is that they are stout-bodied and characterized by many spines and hairs. Many have cervical gills. The tails of the adults have only one segment, and the wings lie relatively flat, or at a slight angle over the abdomen.

The Nemouridae are the most common stoneflies in most of the Rockies, and in "The Stoneflies (Plecoptera) of the Rocky Mountains," Richard W. Baumann, Arden R. Gaufin, and Rebecca F. Surdick write, "This family is very important from an ecological standpoint because they are often the dominant primary consumers in flowing water ecosystems. They are detritovores and often act as shredders of heterotrophic material, such as leaves, that enter the ecosystem from outside."

One of the first life histories of a stonefly was done by Chenfu Francis Wu while at Cornell University in 1921 and 1922. The species was *Nemoura vallicularia,* now known as *Soyedina vallicularia,* which ranges from eastern Canada south to Pennsylvania and west to Michigan. Wu raised captive nymphs of this species in small vials stopped with bolting silk in the brook that flowed through The Glen by the Ithaca home of Professor James G. Needham, an authority on aquatic insects. The nymphs ate only elm leaves and went through 22 instars before emergence began on March 29. Wu reported, "The period of transformation extends from the middle of March to the first of May, with the greater majority emerging during the first half of April. Early in the period of transformation, more males are found but later on the condition is reversed and the females become dominant."

Emergence, Wu reported, occurred between 9 a.m. and 5 p.m., and took place on the vertical surface of any object above the water. Adults were active only on warm, sunny days. Otherwise they remained in damp, sandy places. Mating occurred about a week after emergence and took place during the middle of the day. The males measured 8 millimeters from the head to the tip of the wings, the females 12.5 millimeters.

The Taeniopterygidae

There are 30 members of this family of medium-sized (15 millimeters or less) stoneflies. They are dark brown or blackish and have long antennae and short tails. The giveaway in identifying the Taeniopterygidae is that the second tarsal segment is the same length as or longer than the first segment, as shown in Figure 3–4. Another identifying point is that the wing cases on the nymph tend to diverge from the body axis. Still another point, according to "The Stoneflies (Plecoptera) of the Rocky Mountains," is that the nymphs usually curl up when preserved in alcohol. Ken Stewart says that "the nymphs are debris inhabitors. They are very seldom found in open water among gravelly substrates."

To many Eastern anglers, the "Early Brown Stones" of this family are very important in the weeks following the traditional opening day on

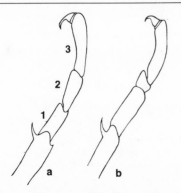

Figure 3–4. Tarsal segments of Euholognathe nymphs.
(*a*) Taeniopterygidae. (*b*) Nemouridae.

April 1. The species that most anglers probably imitate is *Strophopteryx fasciata,* which emerges from mid-March to late April in Connecticut and ranges from Quebec down to North Carolina and westward to Kansas and Minnesota. It is active during the day. In his *New Streamside Guide,* Art Flick gives a pattern for the Early Brown Stone wet fly and notes that "it is important to fishermen because it seems to be the first aquatic insect in which trout show a real interest." In *Nymphs,* Ernest Schwiebert says that sometimes the fly "is more important than the highly touted mayflies of early season."

The nymph of *S. fasciata* is a splendid, elegant insect. White on the ventral surfaces and brown, with just the slightest flush of pink or red, on the back of the abdomen, it has, when you look at it through a magnifying glass, the most marvelous little series of bulges between the tight

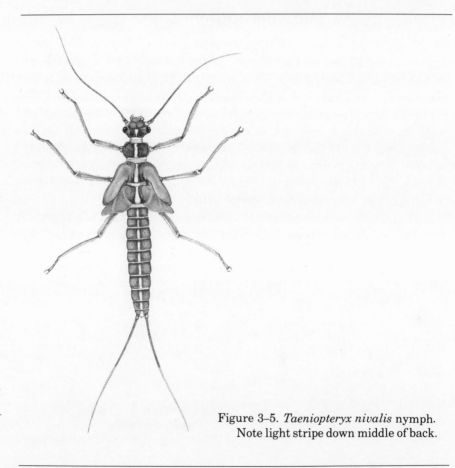

Figure 3–5. *Taeniopteryx nivalis* nymph.
Note light stripe down middle of back.

sutures outlining the abdominal segments. In essence the nymph looks rather like a Hungarian count wearing a constricting series of minicorsets.

A very similar species is *Taeniopteryx nivalis* (Figure 3–5), which is immediately recognizable in the nymphal stage by the yellow or light tan stripe that runs down the middle of the back from the head to the end of the abdomen. This species is found from the Canadian Maritime provinces south to Pennsylvania and west to Minnesota. It has also been reported from Idaho, Oregon, and northern California. In Connecticut, emergence occurs from late February into early April.

SYSTELLOGNATHA

The Perlidae

The family Perlidae numbers 40 species. The paraglossae are rounded, and all three thoracic segments bear finely branched gills. The Perlidae is an important family for many fishermen who are familiar with these so-called big golden stones. A number of the nymphs are beautifully patterned in brown and yellow, such as those of *Paragnetina immarginata,* which is found in the East, those of *Phasganophora capitata,* found in the East and Middle West, and those of members (or former members) of the genus *Acroneuria,* found all across the country (Figure 3–6). They are the tigers of the stonefly world; with their flattened bodies and well-developed legs, they live on stony bottoms where they find both prey and shelter. At maturity, the nymphs vary from 1 to 1½ inches long. The life cycle for many Perlidae may take two to three years. In the West, several species, notably *Hesperoperla pacifica* (Figure 3–7) and *Calineuria californica,* both formerly placed in the genus *Acroneuria,* have significant hatches.

The nymphs of the Perlidae rely on their antennae and tails to find prey. H. B. N. Hynes, who observed British perlids preying on mayfly nymphs in the laboratory, reported that the stoneflies "did not appear to be able to see these nymphs, but as soon as they came into contact with the antennae or cerci they pounced on them, worrying them the way a dog worries a rat, after which they were eaten quickly." Errol W. Claire and Robert W. Phillips observed 29 *Hesperoperla pacifica* nymphs attack and kill 10 steelhead eggs and 22 steelhead alevins in 21 days in the laboratory. They reported "one attack, viewed under a dissecting microscope," that involved a 19-millimeter nymph and a 20-millimeter steelhead ale-

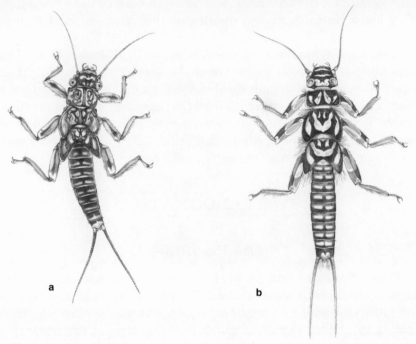

Figure 3–6. The nymphs of two species of Perlidae stoneflies. (*a*) *Paragnetina immarginata.* (*b*) *Phasganophora capitata.*

vin: "The nymph grasped the body of the alevin with its legs. A violent struggle ensued. The nymph then sank one mandible into the eye and the other into the gill region, killing the alevin. For approximately 10 minutes the nymph clung to the alevin, apparently feeding on the aqueous humor from the eye. Then the nymph released the alevin and crawled away."

Nymphs of *H. pacifica* and *Claassenia sabulosa* are "as quick as lizards," Ken Stewart says. Fishing for trout with live nymphs of both of these species, hooked lightly in the cervical membrane beneath the neck, he has watched them scuttle across the stream bottom pulling a split shot behind them like a convict on the lam with his ball and chain.

Stewart and Randall L. Fuller, who studied the food habits of *H. pacifica* and other stonefly nymphs in the upper Gunnison River in Colorado, found them living in the swiftest parts of the river. First-year nymphs fed on chironomid larvae in all months except May, when they took more mayflies. In the fall, second-year nymphs shifted to feeding on much larger numbers and volumes of caddis larvae, and continued to do so into the following May. "This was in spite of the fact that smaller instar chironomid larvae were the most abundant food items in the food complex," reported Fuller and Stewart. In June, before emergence, mature *H. pacifica* nymphs then "shifted back to predominantly chironomid feeding, with a consistent preference indicated."

In the Dolores River in Colorado, Fuller and Stewart found *C. sabulosa* nymphs inhabiting gravelly riffles, with emergence taking place from early August to September. Upon emergence, adults are found beneath rocks on the banks, running like spiders when uncovered. In early summer, the small nymphs fed mainly on mayflies, although they shifted to chironomids and stoneflies as well. In August, the nymphs elected to feed on caddis larvae. Second-year nymphs fed primarily on mayflies and caddis, except in December when chironomids composed 37 percent of the nymphs' gut contents.

Stewart and his students have done two of the most detailed life histories of perlid species. He and George L. Vaught studied *Neoperla clymene,* which is widely distributed in the eastern United States and Canada and which ranges as far to the southwest as Texas, New Mexico, and Arizona.

N. clymene emerges from early June through August in Illinois, with July the peak. The same apparently holds true in Connecticut. In Texas, adults emerge from May through July, with peak emergence in June. Emergence occurs at night and usually starts about an hour after dusk. Transformation from the nymph to the adult fly takes approximately 20 minutes.

Vaught and Stewart report that the adult *N. clymene* "are active at night and secretive by day, hiding under rocks or in vegetation at streamside." Mating takes place at night, and although Vaught and Stewart did not witness oviposition, it is likely that the female drops or washes the egg

Figure 3–7. *Hesperoperla pacifica* adult.

masses into the stream during flight. Most true nocturnal stoneflies, such as *N. clymene,* do not feed as adults, although specimens held in Stewart's laboratory took water from saturated cotton.

The brown, spindle-shaped eggs of *N. clymene* hatch in 25 to 35 days. The nymphs generally take a year to mature and go through as many as 23 instars. There is a spurt of growth in the fall, but little size increase during the winter. Growth resumes in March and continues until hatching. The general color pattern of the nymph is yellowish, with a brown border on the pronotum and brown transverse bands on the abdomen. The adults have a yellow body and brown wings. The females are 18 millimeters long to the tips of the wings, the males 10 millimeters.

The nymphs of *N. clymene* live in riffles. Vaught and Stewart found the standing crop of nymphs in a riffle they studied in the Brazos River to be 225 per square meter in May and about 22 per square meter in July. *N. clymene* is a carnivore and feeds mainly at night. Examination of 433 stomachs disclosed that the nymphs ate mainly the eggs and larvae of the caddis *Cheumatopsyche,* the eggs of *N. clymene* itself, chironomid larvae, *Simulium* larvae, and nematodes.

Stewart and Rosalyn K. Snellen studied *Perlesta placida,* found in Canada from Nova Scotia to Manitoba and in the United States from Vermont south to Florida and westward to Minnesota and Texas. (In *The Stoneflies of Minnesota (Plecoptera),* Philip E. Harden and Clarence E. Mickel reported that "*Perlesta placida* surpasses all other species of Plecoptera found in the state in the number of streams from which it has been collected and in the extent of range within the state.") The nymph of *P. placida* is a tough customer that can survive even in intermittent streams, and in point of fact, Snellen and Stewart studied the species in just such a stream, Clear Creek, in Denton County, Texas.

Adults emerged from May to July when the daily stream temperature approached 68 degrees Fahrenheit. Maximum emergence took place from late May to mid-June. Emergence began one hour after sunset on rocks and debris near the stream. The adults were very secretive and probably hid in trees or high vegetation during the day. They did not feed but took water. In all likelihood, oviposition occurred at night, since "females were found on rocks and vegetation near the [fluorescent] light traps carrying extruded egg masses."

Most hatching in one batch of 797 eggs did not take place until November, and a few *P. placida* continued to hatch until January. One batch did not hatch until a year later, "completely missing one growth-emergence-oviposition season. . . . Thus the eggs seem capable of withstanding long periods of drought," wrote Stewart and Snellen.

Figure 3–8. *Paragnetina media* nymph.

Nymphs that hatched in the fall grew slowly during the winter, but began to grow rapidly in March. The nymphs inhabited leaf packs and other debris in backwater eddies and pools. The dominant streamside trees were cottonwood, sycamore, black willow, and several species of elm.

The young *P. placida* nymphs ate considerable amounts of detritus, then apparently switched to live prey in the leaf packs and debris, with chironomids the predominant food. Before emerging, the nymphs went through an estimated 12 to 16 instars.

The nymphs of *P. placida* are readily recognized because of their many gills and freckled abdomen and thorax. The thorax and legs of the adult are brown, the abdomen yellowish, and the wings brown. The adult female measures 14 millimeters in length, the male 8.5 millimeters.

D. C. Tarter and L. A. Krumholz and others have worked on aspects of the life history of *Paragnetina media* (Figure 3–8), one of the most widely distributed stoneflies in North America, ranging from the Canadian Maritime provinces down to North Carolina and westward to Missouri and Saskatchewan. The immature nymphs of this species are easy to recognize: Covered with long hairs that trap detritus, they look as though they could use a haircut and shave. The legs are also heavily haired. Interestingly, a species of chironomid fly larva sometimes lives in gelatinous cases attached to the nymph of *P. media,* and dines on the detritus caught in the hairs.

In color, the nymphs of *P. media* vary from light to dark brown. The top of the abdomen is uniformly brown, and mature nymphs, which usually lose their long-haired coat, begin to show contrasting color patterns, sometimes of a slightly orange hue on the thorax and head. The length of the body reaches almost an inch.

P. media has sometimes been found in ponds and lakes as well as streams, and can tolerate waters that are too warm or polluted for other stoneflies. In fact, we have collected specimens from a truly grungy stream, Furnace Brook, in Croton-on-Hudson, New York. There, amid old tires, junked refrigerators, rusting cans, and other artifacts of so-called civilization, *P. media* nymphs thrive beneath the stones in rapids.

The nymphs feed upon mayflies, caddis, diptera, and other stoneflies. The life cycle of the species probably takes two years to complete. In Kentucky, emergence takes place from May 6 to August 12, while peak emergence in Wisconsin appears to be in early June. The process of emergence itself apparently takes place in the evening. The adult looks like a small dark *Acroneuria* with wings of a smoky, dark brown color.

The Chloroperlidae

There are 60-odd members of this family in the United States and Canada. The nymphs differ from those of other families in the Systellognatha, according to "The Stoneflies (Plecoptera) of the Rocky Mountains," by their "short cerci, lack of distinct color patterns, rounded wing pads and complete absence of external gills. The body is tubular-shaped and bristled; well adapted to burrowing in the fine gravel of streambeds." The adults are small to medium-sized, and are often yellow or light green in color. It is possible to key out the adults, but the nymphs are difficult.

But don't let that trouble you. We showed Ken Stewart the dry fly imitation of a Chloroperlidae, species unknown, by Dave McNeese (the pattern is given in chapter 8), and Ken replied that "since McNeese reports this little Yellow Stone emerging from mid-June into August, a very long period, the fly is probably not one species but numerous species of *Alloperla*. Most yellow species of this genus have recently been divided into several genera, including *Triznaka, Sweltsa, Suwallia,* and *Neaviperla.*" All little Yellow Sallies look alike, Ken maintained, "and the trout probably can't tell the difference. At Quartz Creek, a tributary of the Gunnison in Colorado, the primary habitat of adult *Alloperla* is in the willows. In Alaska it is in both willows and alder. *Alloperla* is day active, and it's best to fish the little Yellow Sally or green imitations under the willows, near bank undercuts and the margins of streams where willow limbs hang over and where trout may be waiting in the shade. The little female flies also flutter above the edges of the riffles and may be out over the middle of a riffle."

Asked about the nymphs, Stewart said, "I would suggest fishing a mature yellow nymph, a dark brown yellow or a uniform dark yellow with not much pattern. Prior to emergence, the nymphs of *Alloperla* definitely move to shallow water along the edge. They also drift at fairly high rates, which is not yet in the literature." In the Gunnison during the months of July and August, he explained, "*Suwallia, Sweltsa,* and *Triznaka* appear in the drift pulse just after sunset, very evenly distributed in the water 10 centimeters above the bottom. They appear in the drift just before they emerge and at no other time. We assume they emerge early in the morning or late in the evening."

The Perlodidae

This family includes about 100 species. The nymphs are generally described, says Ken Stewart, as "gill-less, waxy, and relatively non-hairy." There is wide variation in size. Some of the larger Perlodidae are as big as some of the Perlidae, but generally speaking the body and legs are not as flattened, as shown here in the illustration of *Hydroperla crosbyi* (Figure 3–9).

The nymph of *Isoperla bilineata* is very important for anglers over much of North America. This species ranges from Quebec south to North Carolina and westward to Colorado and Manitoba. The adult female is 14 millimeters long from the head to the end of the wings, the male 10 millimeters long. The nymph very much resembles a half-pint *Acroneuria, Calineuria californica,* or *Hesperoperla pacifica,* except that it has three dark stripes running the length of the yellow abdomen.

"The nymphs make their most rapid growth from January to April," T. H. Frison reported. "Their size groups as well as seasonal adjustments indicate a life cycle of one year." Emergence in Illinois begins by the end of March and peaks in mid-May, observed Frison. "Very few specimens are encountered after the end of June," he wrote. "*Bilineata* is therefore a true member of the spring fauna. It is essentially nocturnal and adults are often found in numbers at lights. During the day they may be beaten with a net from vegetation bordering rivers or captured while resting in protected places."

The Western angler would do well to take special note of *Isoperla fulva,* both the nymph and adult. Ken Stewart and Stanley W. Szczytko found *I. fulva* to be "the most common western *Isoperla,* from the widest range of lotic [stream] habitat types." It occurs in Arizona, California,

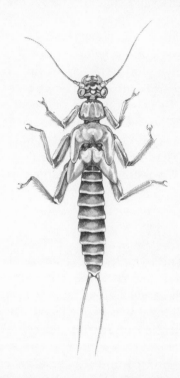

Figure 3–9. *Hydroperla crosbyi* nymph.

Colorado, Idaho, Montana, Nevada, New Mexico, Oregon, Utah, Washington, and Wyoming. In Canada, *I. fulva* is found in Alberta and British Columbia. The species occurs in high- and low-elevation streams, in temporary streams, in stony rivers, and even in the sluggish rivers of the Gunnison system of Colorado.

The life cycle of *I. fulva* lasts for a year. Fuller and Stewart found that in October the newly hatched nymphs primarily ate plant material, with filamentous algae composing almost half the diet. In December, they began to feed on chironomids and mayflies, and in May and June, just prior to emergence, they primarily ate chironomids. The mature male nymph is 11 to 12 millimeters long, the female 13 to 15 millimeters. There is a large U-shaped yellow area between the compound eyes; the pronotum is dark brown except for a median yellow stripe; the abdomen is yellow with three longitudinal stripes: two wide dark brown lateral stripes and one narrow median light brown stripe. The general body color of the adult male and female is light to medium brown. Emergence occurs from early May to August, depending on latitude, but peak numbers of the flies are to be found from mid-June to early July in the central Rockies.

The Peltoperlidae

There are 13 species in this family. The nymphs are immediately recognizable because they look like miniature cockroaches. The Peltoperlidae have been neglected by anglers, perhaps because they are entirely missing in the Middle West, but imitations of the nymphs can be very effective on East- and West-Coast streams. Stark and Stewart have just published a revision of the Peltoperlidae genera, with illustrations of nymphs of each genus.

The species *Yoraperla brevis* occurs in abundance in mountain streams from British Columbia to California and Montana. Dark brown in color, it is the smallest Pacific Coast member of its genus; the body length of the mature nymph is only 4 to 6 millimeters. The nymph apparently feeds mainly on algae. The life history of the species has yet to be revealed, but perhaps some of what we know about an eastern species, *Peltoperla maria* (Figure 3–10), may be applicable to *Y. brevis.*

P. maria ranges from Vermont to northern Georgia, but has not yet been found west of the Appalachians. The mahogany-colored nymph is extremely abundant in many streams of the southern Appalachians, with reported peak densities of more than 500 per square meter. It is the dominant stonefly species in western North Carolina trout streams, and it is abundant in many streams in New York, Connecticut, and Massachusetts. A very similar species, *P. arcuata,* ranges from Quebec to Virginia.

Figure 3–10. *Peltoperla* nymph.

P. maria is almost always found in leaf packs and detritus in areas with some current. It apparently does not like to live in pools. The nymphs are often so numerous in a leaf pack that it is easy to find specimens that have recently molted; they are whitish to light tan in color.

Trout are well aware of the nymphs of *P. maria;* they will actually nose around in leaf litter to get at them. Take note of the fact that the nymphs are also night drifters. Emergence occurs in June in New York, and until that time nymphal imitations on size 12 to 18 hooks can be very effective when fished down through riffles or in quieter backwaters. We describe just such an imitation tied by Paul Schmookler in chapter 8.

The Pteronarcyidae

This very important stonefly family has 10 species divided into 3 genera, *Pteronarcella, Pteronarcys,* and *Allonarcys.*

Pteronarcella badia and *P. regularis* are found in the West, with *P. badia* common in Alaska. This species probably has a 2-year life cycle and reaches about an inch in length. Superficially, the dark brown nymphs look very much like the half-grown nymphs of *Pteronarcys* and *Allonarcys.* Stewart and Fuller found *P. badia* nymphs inhabiting debris in the slower waters of both the Dolores and Gunnison rivers in Colorado. They eat detritus, moss, and some animal matter, primarily chironomid larvae and mayfly nymphs. Peak emergence on the upper Gunnison was in late June.

By far the most celebrated member of the family is *Pteronarcys californica,* the salmonfly whose praises we sang in chapter 1. This species has a 3- and, in some instances, possibly a 4-year life cycle. It is to be found in the swiftest parts of rivers throughout much of the West.

In the Dolores River, Stewart and Fuller found that *P. californica* had its peak emergence from late May to mid-June. The nymphs of the species (Figure 3–11) ate large amounts of detritus. "Probably it is a generalist, feeding on detritus or living plants as they are encountered," Stewart and Fuller wrote. "The sluggish movements of *P. californica* nymphs would further suggest that the species could not be an effective predator." The mature nymphs are about 2 inches long. The adults have an orange-colored abdomen.

Charles E. Brooks, the Montana angler and author, was so curious about the nymphs of *P. californica* that he spent time underwater observing them in the Madison River. "I found that the *Pteronarcys* nymphs feed twice every 24 hours," Charlie says. "I'd see them come out from under

Figure 3–11. *Pteronarcys californica* nymph.

the rocks where they live to feed on the algae on top of the rocks. First the smaller nymphs would come out, then the bigger ones, and finally the biggest. Then I tried to find out why the nymphs were feeding when they did. In the summer, they liked to feed at 58 degrees Fahrenheit and generally knocked off when it reaches 62 degrees. Then, when the water cooled down in the late afternoon, they fed again. In the fall, when the water cools, 52 degrees will bring them out to feed." Back in 1927, Richard Muttkowski, who studied the nymphs in the Yellowstone River, said, "The roving habits of this species make it a favorable food item for trout, more so than any other species."

Jay W. Richardson and Arden R. Gaufin of the University of Utah, who fed leaves and prepared fish meal to *P. californica* nymphs in their laboratory, reported, "The nymphs usually lie in crevices with antennae protruding and waving from side to side. Then the antennae contact food material, the nymphs rush out and grab the food with the maxillae. When actively searching for food, the nymphs move over rocks slowly, feeding as they go, the antennae continuously moving to and fro." Emergence takes place when the water temperature approaches 60 degrees Fahrenheit, and it moves upstream as the water warms. The best place to fish the dry salmonfly of *P. californica* is at the head of the hatch. Before the

Figure 3–12. *Allonarcys biloba* nymph.

head of the hatch arrives, the big nymph imitation fished close to the bottom will do well, because the trout are ready to pounce on the nymphs migrating toward shore to emerge.

When planning to fish the salmonfly hatch, it is always best to call ahead, because weather conditions can hasten or prolong emergence, and emergence varies from river to river. On the Rogue River in Oregon, emergence usually begins in mid-May and stops, upstream, at the end of June. On the Madison, emergence usually occurs between mid-June and mid-July, and on the Yellowstone, it begins near Livingston during the last week in June and ends about August 1 in the higher elevations of Yellowstone Park.

A closely related species is *P. princeps*. The nymphs of this species are common in creeks and rivers in California, Oregon, and Washington, but rare in the Rockies. The adults have smoky wings, and emergence takes place from April through June.

There are two other *Pteronarcys* species: the transcontinental *P. dorsata* mentioned in chapter 1, and *P. pictetii,* which is found from Kansas to Georgia. *P. dorsata* nymphs mainly live in the detritus in eddies below rapids. The nymphs of both *P. dorsata* and *P. pictetii* are, of course, similar in size and color to those of *P. californica* and *P. princeps*. The same is also true of all the species of *Allonarcys* that were formerly placed in the genus *Pteronarcys,* except that the *Allonarcys* species have lateral hooks on the abdomen (Figure 3–12). The presence or absence of lateral hooks doesn't mean a thing to a trout, although trying to separate one *Allonarcys* from another can sometimes drive you crazy because the hooks don't always bend at the angles shown in the keys. The *Allonarcys* species are *A. comstocki,* which ranges from New England south to Virginia; *A. biloba,* from Quebec south to Georgia; *A. scotti,* from Tennessee to Georgia; and *A. proteus,* from Quebec south to Virginia.

These species emerge in May and June. The adults appear to be nocturnal, and although the numbers emerging are nowhere near those of *Pteronarcys californica,* the dry fly imitation can be a killer at night. And as we noted in chapter 1, you can't go wrong anywhere fishing the big dark nymph, no matter whether it's supposed to be *Pteronarcys, Allonarcys,* or even *Pteronarcella.*

WE'VE THROWN a lot of information at you. We have no intention of complicating matters, though sooner or later the really serious fly fisherman is going to get interested in stoneflies, species by species. However, if you're not that interested and want your stoneflies simplified, or even oversimplified, here's a table encapsulating the key points about the nymphs of all nine Plecoptera families in the U. S. and Canada.

**INSTANT-EXPERT
OVER-SIMPLIFIED NYMPH RECOGNITION TABLE**

FAMILY	HOOK SIZE	TAILS AND ANTENNAE	ABDOMEN
Leuctridae Capniidae Nemouridae Taeniopterygidae	10–18	Light to dark brown	Light to dark brown
Perlidae	4–16	Brown	Brown and yellow. Abdomen flattened. Belly paler
Chloroperlidae	10–18	Yellow to light brown, green	Yellow, green, brown. Abdomen tube-like
Perlodidae	6–14	Brown, yellow	Brown and yellow. Much like Perlidae but body not as flattened and not hairy
Peltoperlidae	12–18	Mahogany brown, short tails	Mahogany brown. Body roach-like, flattened
Pteronarcyidae	2–8	Dark brown	Dark brown. Belly pale. Oval-shaped. Gill tufts on first 2 or 3 abdominal segments

THORAX	WING PADS	OTHER	FAMILY
Light to dark brown	Light to dark brown	Usually in detritus; many emerge in winter and early spring, some in summer, a few in fall	Leuctridae Capniidae Nemouridae Taeniopterygidae
Same color as belly. With branched gills	Same as top of abdomen, often strikingly patterned	Stony bottoms, gravel riffles. Emergence in late spring to midsummer. Some drift	Perlidae
Yellow, green, brown. No gills	Rounded, no patterns	Well adapted to gravel habitat. Emergence early spring and summer. Drifts before emergence	Chloroperlidae
Brown and yellow. If gills are present, they are unbranched	Often strikingly patterned	Wide variety of habitats	Perlodidae
Mahogany brown	Mahogany brown	Abundant in leaf packs with some current. Avoids pools. East and West coast only. Night drifter	Peltoperlidae
Dark brown with gill tufts	Dark brown to black	Likes bottom of swift Western rivers. In Midwest and East, below rapids and in leaf packs with current. Nymphs curl in hand	Pteronarcyidae

4

IMITATING THE STONEFLY NYMPH

An artificial Stone Fly
nymph will take fish at any time of the year.

—Joe Brooks, *Trout Fishing*

THERE IS JUST SOMETHING about a stonefly nymph that prompts many fly tyers to go all out. Ted Niemeyer, Poul Jorgensen, and Yaz Yamashito have concocted incredibly realistic imitations; Yaz even goes so far as to put two claws on each leg. Considering that some of these nymphs can take up to 10 hours to tie, it's no wonder that most are framed rather than fished.

Ultrarealistic imitations are marvelous to look at, and Niemeyer found that the trout agreed— they *looked* more often than they hit. "The nymphs were too realistic," Niemeyer says. "They were too stiff. Realism is motion as well as design."

What Ted says is true. Size, shape, and color are important, but motion—action—is critical. Anyone tying a nymph should try to make it give the impression that it is alive rather than merely lifelike. The nymphs we'll show you how to tie in this chapter imitate the natural and look alive in the water. First we're going to deal with the anatomy of the nymph and the materials used to imitate the tails, abdomen, thorax (wing cases, pronotum, legs, and gills) and the antennae. We will also deal with weighted and unweighted nymphs. In all of this, we will be giving you the benefit of our experience and the experience of others who have done a lot of tying. Personally, we have experimented with many stonefly nymphs, both alive and artificial, and—because one of the utter joys in tying is that there is always some new wrinkle—by the time you read this, we may well have galloped on, shouting hurrahs for some new material or technique. But we're not dealing in absolutes. Do what suits *you*.

The Hook

Let's start with the hook. Suppose we're going to tie a mature nymph of *Pteronarcys californica, P. dorsata,* or *Allonarcys biloba.* They all look very much the same, and all measure about 2 inches in length. Two hooks come to mind, the Mustad #79580 and #9575; the #79580 is designated 4XL, while the #9575 is a 6XL. Of the two, #9575 is the more desirable; it has a longer shank, a Limerick bend (one of the best for holding fish), and a looped eye that helps form a flat base for the head. The looped eye also prevents the leader from being cut once the nymph is attached.

To be sure, other manufacturers make long-shanked hooks, and if you find them suitable, by all means use them. Frankly, despite all the talk about English hooks, we think Mustad still makes the best. Moreover, Mustad hooks are readily available in supply houses.

Now the question—to weight or not to weight the nymph? There are arguments pro and con. An unweighted nymph won't get to the stream bottom unless you add split shot or a lead strip, while a weighted nymph will bounce along the bottom. But since an unweighted imitation nymph weighs about the same as a natural nymph, reason dictates that it will have better action than a weighted nymph.

The angler fishing an unweighted nymph often adds split shot or lead foil on the leader above the nymph, applying more lead the deeper and faster the water. The disadvantage of this is that it gives you more hangups, both underwater and in your mind. An experienced nymph fisherman knows that any hesitation during line flow downstream may mean that a trout has taken the nymph; unfortunately, most such hesitations are caused by the weighted leader hanging up on rocks or logs, and it tries your patience to be striking at the bottom instead of the fish. Still, patience is its own reward, and that fifth or sixth snag may be a trout. Even so, if you're going to fish the unweighted nymph there's a better way of adding weight to the leader; it's a Lefty Kreh idea that we've modified slightly, as follows: when you tie the nymph on the leader, leave 3 to 6 inches of tippet material extending beyond your knot. Press a split shot on the end and start fishing. Lefty burns the tip of the leader so that the split shot stays on; we don't do this. Then, should the split shot become snagged or wedged in a crevice, a slight tug will usually free the nymph.

For really deep, fast water, some anglers weight both the nymph and the leader, and are successful. But if you do this, remember to lob, rather than cast, your line if you don't want a hook in the neck.

If your preference is for weighting nymphs, you should use the added weight to help form the underbody properly.

Weighting Nymphs

There are various ways to add weight to a nymph while simultaneously forming a properly proportioned underbody. Many stoneflies, notably the Perlidae, have flat bodies that enable them to move about the bottom freely. Others, such as the Pteronarcyidae, have oval bodies. Still others seem to have a shape somewhere between the two—a flat oval. Here are some methods we use to form the weighted underbodies of these nymphs.

Flat-Bodied Nymphs (Figure 4–1) For most of our weighting methods we use a lead fuse wire, which is available in the following sizes:

1 amp—diameter .016 inch (for hook sizes 10 and 12)
2 amp—diameter .024 inch (for hook sizes 6 and 8)
3 amp—diameter .036 inch (for hook sizes 2 and 4)

In making the flat-bodied nymph, the hook first is clamped in the vise, and tying thread is wrapped along the entire length of the shank to insure better support of the wire to be attached.

Two pieces of lead wire are angle cut at both ends so that they measure slightly less than the hook shank. This is done because enough room must be left on the hook shank, especially at the tail area, for securing other materials.

Take one piece of the cut lead wire and hold it to the shank on the far side of the hook. The angled cuts made at each end should taper in to the hook shank. Holding the wire in place with your free hand, wind the tying thread around both the wire and the shank with your other hand;

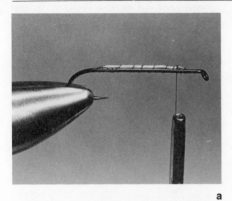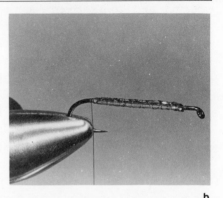

a

b

Figure 4–1. Weighting flat-bodied nymphs. (*a*) Tying first lead wire to side of hook shank. (*b*) Both lead wire strips tied to hook shank.

use enough wraps of thread so that the wire doesn't slip from its position. Now take the other piece of lead wire and secure it to the shank on the near side of the hook. Again use enough turns of thread to hold the wire securely in place. If one or both of the wires does slip out of place, just pinch the hook shank on the top and bottom with a pair of flat-nosed pliers so that the wires are once more aligned.

Next, take a dubbing needle and apply a liberal amount of head cement to the windings; also, take a few more turns of thread back and forth across the hook shank. The lead wire should be tied in strongly enough so that it doesn't revolve or move out of position when other materials are tied in over it. As you can see, adding lead wire strips to the sides of the hook shank gives a very flat appearance.

Oval-Shaped Nymphs (Figure 4–2) Forming the lead underbody for an oval-shaped nymph is the easiest way of weighting a nymph. After determining the proper diameter needed, simply break off a section of fuse wire about 5 inches long. With the hook in the vise and the thread spiraled to the shank, leave the thread dangling at the bend (*a*).

Next, take one end of the lead wire between your left thumb and forefinger, and the remainder in your right hand; hold the wire diagonally across the hook shank, just forward of the bend where the thread was left dangling. Then, with the end of the lead wire held tightly between your left thumb and forefinger, wind the wire around the shank in connecting spirals to a point one-eighth of an inch from the eye of the hook (*b*). If the

the spirals are loose or slightly open just push them together with your thumbs and forefingers. Break or cut off the excess lead wire at both ends.

Now take the thread dangling at the hook bend and wind a number of turns around the hook shank just in back of the lead wire spirals near the bend; wind enough turns to make a smooth, natural taper from the lead wire to the hook shank. When you have done this, wind the thread forward and through the spirals of lead wire toward the eye of the hook, winding enough turns of thread just in front of the lead wire so that the eye end, like the rear, forms a natural taper from lead wire to shank. Now, with your dubbing needle, dab a liberal amount of head cement to the lead wire. Work the thread back and forth across the lead wire three or four times more, finally returning the thread to its position just before the bend.

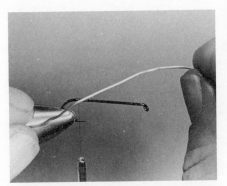
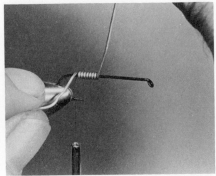

a

b

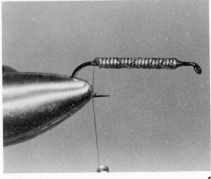

c

Figure 4–2. Weighting oval-shaped nymphs. (*a*) Lead wire positioned before winding. (*b*) Spiraling lead wire around shank. (*c*) The completed oval lead wire underbody.

Flat Oval-Shaped Nymphs (Figure 4–3) If you can form both a flat lead underbody and an oval one, making a flat oval-shaped body is relatively simple, since it involves combining the methods for both. Depending on how much weight you want, there are actually two ways to go about it. The first and obviously easiest method is simply to form the oval shape by winding spirals of lead wire around the hook shank and then mashing them flat with a pair of flat-nosed pliers (*a*). The resulting shape, although somewhat flat, does retain some semblance of an oval because the wire was originally wound completely around the hook shank.

The second method for making the flat oval-shaped body is first to form the flat-bodied shape and then to wrap spirals of lead wire around it. This method uses more lead wire, since you not only have two pieces lashed to the sides, but the oval spirals as well (*b,c*).

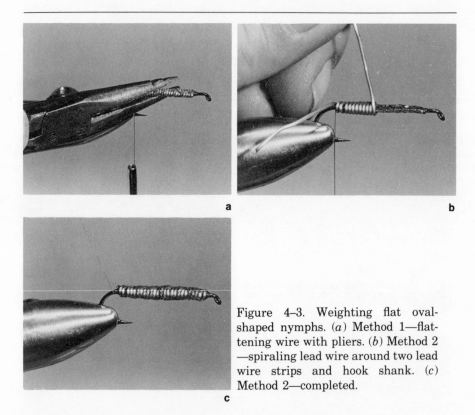

Figure 4–3. Weighting flat oval-shaped nymphs. (*a*) Method 1—flattening wire with pliers. (*b*) Method 2 —spiraling lead wire around two lead wire strips and hook shank. (*c*) Method 2—completed.

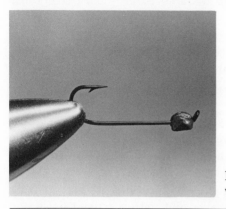

Figure 4–4. Split shot added for weight.

BY USING any of the foregoing methods, or a combination of them, you can get a variety of shapes for the underbody, thus allowing for greater imitation of any specific natural nymph.

Besides using lead wire, you can also make a weighted underbody by using a small sinker and hammering it flat. Obviously you can't use too big a sinker, or you'll be pounding it all day long; the long, quarter-ounce and half-ounce variety are ideal. When you have hammered the sinker into a flattened shape, you will need a pair of heavy-duty scissors or shears to cut it to the shape of a stonefly body slightly smaller than the hook you are tying on.

If you happen to own some apparatus for melting lead, such as that used by anglers who make their own jigs, it's easy enough to pour some molten lead onto a concrete floor or surface and let it cool and harden. The resulting lead flakes are flat and yet thick enough in most instances to form the proper shape for the flat oval underbody. At worst, if the flakes do need some pounding with a hammer, it takes only a little effort to achieve the desired diameter; the method is much quicker than starting with a sinker.

When the flakes have been shaped to a properly sized underbody, they are lashed to the top of the hook shank with enough turns of thread to prevent them from revolving or moving when other materials are tied over them. A liberal amount of head cement is also applied.

Still another way to weight a nymph is to press a small split shot onto the hook to serve as the head. This split-shot nymph is tied upside down (Figure 4–4). Be sure to place the hook shank deep into the split, so that most of the weight of the shot will be on the underside of the finished nymph. This causes the hook point to ride up, the way it does on a jig.

When using split shot for the head, make sure that you use the proper size shot. A nymph with an oversized head would appear unnatural. There used to be an availability of very small split shot for hook sizes down to 10 or 12, but we haven't been able to find any on the market lately; the smallest shots we have been able to locate are those designated "B," or "BB," which will accommodate size 6 (BB) and 8 (B) hooks.

Unweighted Underbodies If your preference is for unweighted nymphs, there are a couple of ways to form the flat underbody. The conventional way is to use acetate floss and build a body on the hook shank the way you would for such flies as the Black Ghost or Grey Ghost. After the body has been formed, acetone, which reacts with acetate floss, is applied. The body can then be mashed flat with a pair of flat-nosed pliers.

Another method—and one we prefer to use—is to make a slightly smaller-than-natural sized nymph body from a sheet of plastic. The plastic we use may be from .018 to .024 inches thick, depending on the size hook it is to be used on. The larger nymphs require a little more thickness. Such sheets of plastic can be found in hobby shops; you may even have some lying around the house. X-ray film is fine for forming this type of underbody. Cutting an individual piece of plastic to shape can be a nuisance. In order to save time, we keep basic shape-models for various hook sizes on hand, and whenever we want to make some underbodies we simply put a basic model on a large piece of plastic and trace the outline with a pencil; then it's just a matter of minutes to cut a piece to the exact shape needed for that number hook.

In addition to forming your own nymph body from plastic, there is a

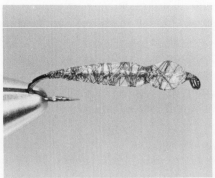

Figure 4–5. Flat, plastic underbody secured with thread.

product called "Nymphform" on the market. It is packaged by size, and contains approximately three dozen precut and shaped plastic bodies in a package, all ready to go onto your hook shank. The preshaped plastic underbodies are placed on top of a prethreaded hook shank. (Here again, the shank is covered with thread to give the slippery plastic more support.) There should be enough space near the bend and just before the eye to allow other materials to be tied on and finished off.

As with the pieces of lead wire, the plastic underbody is well lashed to the shank with many back and forth windings of thread (Figure 4–5), and is well coated with head cement so that it doesn't move or revolve when other materials are being tied on and over it.

A VERY RECENT development by Partridge, the English hook manufacturer, is the Draper "Flat Bodied" nymph hook. Developed by Keith Draper of New Zealand, the hook features a split shank that angles outward at the center and comes back together near the bend. It can also be weighted. We haven't had a chance to try it ourselves, but the connections at the joining seem well formed.

A final tip on weighted and unweighted nymphs: If you tie both—and many tyers do—color code them for quick selection. A friend of ours, Ken Gerhardt of Peekskill, New York, codes his unweighted nymphs by tying in a few turns of orange thread in the head, while his weighted nymphs all have black heads.

Tails

The tails for stonefly nymphs have been made from every conceivable material. Peccary, porcupine bristle, the face whiskers of animals, quill stems from feathers, and monofilament are often used, and successfully so; to our thinking, however, these materials are just a little too stiff to have proper action. The tails of the natural nymph are not hard; they are soft, and can move and undulate in the current.

The guard hairs from the tail and back of the woodchuck make fine tails for small nymphs. Moose hair has flexibility, but is not as durable as we would like. The biots, or fibers cut from the short side of a goose- or turkey-wing flight feather, make excellent nymph tails. They are surprisingly tough, naturally tapered, and move well enough in the current; many do not have to be dyed, but should you find dyeing necessary, they take to it readily.

For some reason or other, rubber strands are apparently used only to make the tail of the Bitch Creek nymph. Nevertheless, rubber strands are excellent, and given the success of the Bitch Creek nymph, we don't understand why this material isn't used on more patterns.

The Abdomen

All sorts of materials are used for the abdomens of nymph imitations, including woven floss, monofilament, latex, Swannundaze, and, of course, a variety of furs and furlike synthetics ribbed with tinsel, fine wire, monofilament, and thread. So far we haven't found the absolutely perfect abdominal material, so let's look at the advantages and disadvantages of the materials in use.

Woven floss can impart a very lifelike appearance, and is durable. Its big drawback, in our opinion, is that the nymphs are too hard, and the trout quickly eject them.

Quill sheathing, peeled off a peacock, goose, or turkey feather shaft is also a little hard, but can be made softer and more flexible with a bit of effort. Take a goose flight feather, the kind they used to write with many years ago. You will find that the outer covering of the center quill is made of a smooth, hard substance, while the center has a soft pithy texture through most of the quill, except for the butt end, which is hollow.

In order to obtain a strip of this "sheathing" or outer covering, it is best to first soak the quill in hot water for an hour or so. This will soften it. Then, a nick is made, with a razor blade or scalpel, in the quill stem near the top part where it is narrowest. Once you have nicked and freed a small section of the quill, the protruding portion is grasped with a pair of pliers and the entire strip is peeled from the quill shaft. Figure 4–6 shows the method for obtaining a quill sheathing strip. With feathers from birds such as the goose and turkey, you will end up with a tapered quill, one narrower at the top than at the bottom. With a peacock feather, the quill will be straight, with no visible taper.

We generally peel off 10-inch strips of peacock quill and scrape and sandpaper any pith off the inside of the sheath. We then dye the strips, usually orange or yellow. After this the strips are tied to the hook shank near the bend, and are spiraled forward in connecting turns till the abdomen is formed. After an underbody has been formed, the back, or topside, of the quill is marked with a brown, dark brown, or black Pantone marking pen so that the nymph has a dark back and a light belly.

Several years ago we sent a *Pteronarcys californica* nymph made from quill to Hartt Wixom in Salt Lake City, who reported that it was lethal. If you think about it, quill is probably the most natural looking

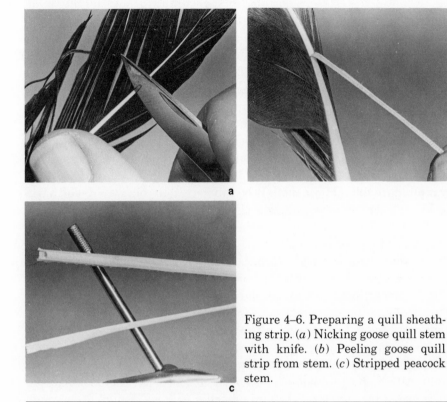

Figure 4–6. Preparing a quill sheathing strip. (*a*) Nicking goose quill stem with knife. (*b*) Peeling goose quill strip from stem. (*c*) Stripped peacock stem.

material you can use; it resembles the chitinous exoskeleton of the natural nymph. Wrapping the quill over a fur or wool underbody makes the abdomen of the nymph imitation look and feel juicy. Yes, we have also made tails, antennae, and legs from quill, but no matter what we did we couldn't make them soft enough.

After the publication of Ernest Schwiebert's *Nymphs,* 20- to 30-pound-test, oval monofilament became the abdominal answer; but, although it is easy to use, it is unnaturally hard. Moreover, it is not wide enough to duplicate the body segments on the larger nymphs.

Latex—the thin, soft, and stretchable rubber material dentists use when they work on your teeth—is a little thin for making nymph bodies, and unless you double it up by using two strips simultaneously, you don't get the segmented effect. As we noted, we use latex for tails, antennae, and legs, and we like it for the abdomen also. But we never tie up too many nymphs with latex because it has a way of rotting in the fly box.

Swannundaze is the trade name for a plastic strip material that is flat on one side and oval on the other. It comes in a variety of colors, both opaque and transparent, and also in clear form. It is wide enough to form the abdomen of the larger nymphs. If it is to be used for smaller nymphs, it can be made narrower by holding it over a steaming tea kettle or under very hot tap water and stretching it. When Swannundaze is to be stretched for the smaller-sized nymphs, a strip about 10 inches long should be held over the steam (or under hot water) and slowly pulled apart until the desired width has been reached; if the material is pulled too fast it will break. We've seen Swannundaze stretched fine enough for tying a number 22 caddis larva. Once the desired width has been reached, the Swannundaze should immediately be submerged in cold water, which will harden and fix the new diameter.

The two of us have a disagreement about Swannundaze: Leiser says it has a yielding quality and that he can actually dent it with his finger-nail. Boyle thinks it's a bit hard, but that if Leiser could combine the shape of Swannundaze with the softness of latex, and then inject this hybrid with chitinous compounds, he might have something. In any event, to the eye, Swannundaze makes a fairly realistic imitation, and it's heavy enough to have a fairly rapid rate of sink.

Various furs, such as muskrat, rabbit, mink, beaver, and otter, used either alone or in a blend, have long been popular for making nymph bodies. Although a fur abdomen, even when ribbed, may not look realistic to the eye, a fuzzy nymph certainly catches fish, as "Polly" Rosborough can attest. Fur nymphs breathe and act alive.

In recent years, many tyers have turned to synthetics, such as Seal-ex and Un-Seal, for nymph bodies; like fur, these materials are also effective. Raw wool is very usable, and chenille has long been a standby; in fact, Izaak Walton first gave the pattern for the Woolly Worm back in 1653, but this imitation didn't become popular in the United States until used as a bass fly in the Ozarks in the 1920s. In *The Practical Fly Fisherman,* A. J. McClane writes that "a fellow by the name of Walter Bales from Kansas City, Missouri, snaffled a prize-winning rainbow on [the Woolly Worm] back in 1935 and passed the pattern on to Don Martinez in West Yellowstone, Montana. At any rate, Don nursed it along, and the Worm became synonymous with Western trouting."

The Woolly Worm is supposed to represent a caterpillar, but Martinez thought it imitated a mayfly nymph because the pulsing, palmered hackles simulated the gills. Yet there can be no doubt that trout often take the big black Woolly Worm for a *Pteronarcys.* In short, the Woolly

Worm has accounted for more fish than any other so-called stonefly pattern. It is for this reason that we have listed it with other patterns later in this chapter.

Segmentation

Swannundaze, quill sheathing, and doubled latex need no segmentation, but fur, wool, yarn, and synthetics require it, not just for added visual appeal but to help keep the nymph from being chewed up. Yet how many times have you seen the fish want the chewed-up nymph!

Popular ribbing materials include copper or brass wire, oval tinsel, fine mylar, Monocord, and thread.

The Thorax

The most important part of the thorax as far as materials are concerned is not the wing pads and pronotum, although many tyers go to extreme lengths to imitate them in size, color, and marking, down to the last detail. No, the most important part of tying a thorax on a nymph is on the underside, where the abdomen ends and to a point just under the head.

Many nymphs have realistic abdomens, such as those made from Swannundaze, quill sheathing, and the like, and this is fine. But with the exception of legs and tails there isn't much room left on a nymph for adding a material that moves, undulates, and pulses, giving the imitation its most important ingredient—lifelikeness. The underside of the thorax gives this opportunity. Here is where we can add the scraggly furs, natural or synthetic, that will add that fish-taking quality to our pattern.

Although most furs and synthetics will do very well for making a nymph thorax, we like to use those that are extra scraggly or fuzzy. Such furs as seal or their imitative substitutes are ideal; so is hare's mask fur. Consider, for example, one of the most effective, time-honored flies ever created, the Gold Ribbed Hare's Ear; although it doesn't imitate anything in particular, it has, like the Woolly Worm, accounted for more fish than any of the standard nymphs or wet flies.

Sometimes, when it's impossible to use the scraggliest of furs or yarns for the thorax, the rough appearance can be attained by poking the under thorax of the finished nymph with a dubbing needle or a dubbing teaser —a tool similar to a dubbing needle except that it has a row of jagged teeth near its working end. The teaser, incidentally, is so effective that you can even rough up a smooth floss body with it.

The wing cases or wing pads of a nymph can be made from a number of feathers, such as mottled turkey, hen saddle feathers, ringneck body feathers, and the like. Only recently, a tool has become available for preshaping these feathers for various sized hooks, so that all you have to do is lay the feather on top of the hook shank and tie it in. The tool we

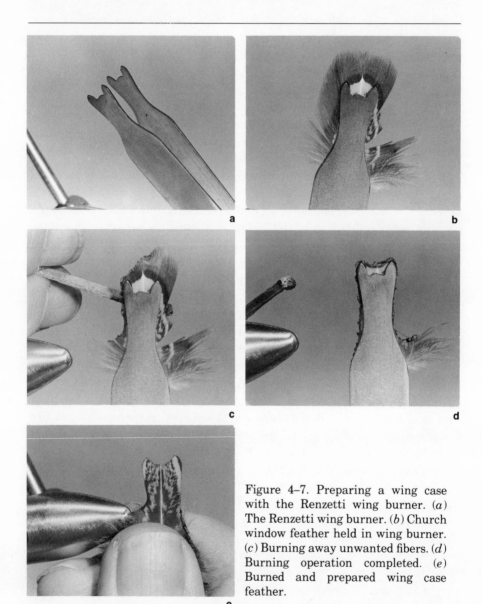

Figure 4–7. Preparing a wing case with the Renzetti wing burner. (a) The Renzetti wing burner. (b) Church window feather held in wing burner. (c) Burning away unwanted fibers. (d) Burning operation completed. (e) Burned and prepared wing case feather.

are referring to is the Renzetti nymph wing case former, invented by Jack Mickievicz of Phoenixville, Pennsylvania. The tool is nothing more than a pair of flat pieces of brass that have been welded together at one end, while the other, working end has been die-cut to the shape of a nymph's wing pads. A feather is inserted between the two tips, and the flame from a match is applied to the exposed portion of the feather, burning away all of the feather that doesn't resemble the wing pad. The entire procedure is shown in Figure 4–7.

Wing pads can also be constructed as a complete unit, in the conventional mayfly nymph manner. This method simply involves tying in a mottled feather such as a turkey wing quill and, after the fur part of the thorax has been completed, folding the feather over and forward and tying it down. The wing pad can also be made of a number of peacock herl fibers, such as Dave Whitlock uses on his Whitlock Black Nymph. Still another method—and one that you'll see used in a pattern shortly upcoming—is the all fur and hair method.

Legs

The most important thing to remember about legs is that on a natural stonefly nymph, they can move. You may have seen some beautifully dressed nymph imitations on which every detail, including the claws at the end, is present. But such legs belong to the fly that is to be framed, not fished; they just do not have enough natural movement in the water, and they are also usually not durable.

The best material you can use for the legs on a nymph imitation are the clumps of feather fibers from such birds as the wood duck, grouse, or partridge, or some of the mottled hen neck or saddle patches. They are soft, can be found in the proper shade of color or dyed perfectly to imitate it, and move and undulate when fished. Of the synthetics, latex trimmed to shape is ideal; and perhaps more crudely but no less effective than feather fibers, rubber strands become very enticing as they throb in a stream current.

The Antennae

The antennae on a nymph are window dressing. They look great and, when made of the right material, such as that used for the tails, add action to the nymph. But a nymph with antennae can be a pain to use because these structures have a knack of getting caught in the leader knot.

Eyes

Eyes are optional. If you want them, fine; but don't go berserk by burning the ends of a piece of monofilament into round balls and then tying in this short section of so-called "eyed mono" on the head. The eyes of stoneflies are not that prominent. A small dab of black lacquer, applied with a small rounded dowel, will do. Niemeyer ties a marvelous hellgrammite until he gets to the eyes. Then on go knotted eyes, and the hellgrammite looks as though it just came from the optician.

So MUCH FOR ALL our pronouncements on materials. Now it's time to show you the step-by-step tying sequences for some fishable stonefly nymphs.

Acroneuria

We use the term *Acroneuria* to include the colorful nymphs that are still included in this genus by the systematists, as well as those species that have lately been given the generic names of *Calineuria, Hesperoperla,* and *Doroneuria.* As Ken Stewart said in chapter 1, if he has to look through a microscope, it can't make a difference to the trout. These stonefly nymphs can be found from coast to coast, and their imitations are valued additions to the fly box. Obviously you can use the tying techniques shown here to simulate nymphs in other families. Just change the colors and select a hook to match the size of the natural.

ACRONEURIA (Figure 4–8)

HOOK SIZE: 6 to 12 (Mustad #79580)
THREAD: Dark brown
TAIL: Two brown goose biots
UNDERBODY: Lead wire or plastic form, over which yellow dubbing is wound the length of the abdomen
ABDOMEN: Transparent brown Swannundaze material
SEGMENTATION: Rib of black Monocord thread
THORAX: Pale amber dubbing (one-half yellow rabbit blended with one-half orange Un-Seal or Seal-ex)
WING CASE: Dark brown mink fur and hair (or similar substitute)
LEGS: Fur fibers of wing case
EYES: Black lacquer (optional)

Insert a size 8 hook in your vise and spiral some dark brown thread onto the shank, terminating at the bend. (Flymaster thread, a pre-waxed size 6/0, is recommended.) We prefer to bend the hook shank into a slight curve with a pair of pliers. This, however, is optional.

Select two dark brown goose biots on the narrow edge of a goose flight feather, and tie one in on each side of the shank so that the two fibers protrude beyond the bend for approximately half an inch (*a*). Tie in the fiber on the far side of the shank first. Once it has been tied in, take one turn of thread around the shank under the butt end, and then bring your thread one more turn around both the fiber and the shank. This will prevent the tail from slipping when you tie in the tail fiber nearest you. Snip off the excess butts.

If the nymph is to be weighted, tie in two strips of lead wire on each side of the hook.

If the nymph is to be unweighted, a plastic form, such as the one shown in the illustration, is lashed to the top of the hook shank.

Two important points to remember when forming the underbody are: (1) to leave adequate space between the bend (where the tails were tied in) and the rear of the lead wire or plastic form. You will need this space to tie in the Swannundaze and ribbing. (2) Be sure to wrap enough thread over (or through) and in front and back of the lead wire or plastic form so that it does not slip or rotate. A liberal amount of head cement over the thread windings will be of help here.

Cut a 5-inch section of black Monocord thread from your spool and tie it in between the tail and lead wire or plastic form.

Cut a 6-inch section of transparent brown Swannundaze and make an angle cut at one end with a scalpel or very sharp knife. Tie the Swannundaze in by its trimmed tip, making sure the flat side is against the shank (*b*). As you take your turns of thread around the Swannundaze to secure it, pull on it slightly so that it will stretch. By stretching it you will be able to make it lie flatter against the shank at its starting point. We actually make our first two turns rearward toward the bend, "programming" our turns so that the Swannundaze will wind properly when it is later needed.

Spin some yellow dubbing (either natural or synthetic will do) onto your thread and wind it forward slightly more than half the shank length (*c,d*). There should be enough to cover the plastic form or lead wire completely to that point.

Apply a coat of clear head cement to the top side of the yellow dubbing to prevent the ink from your Pantone pen from bleeding through to the underside. Take a brown Pantone pen (#464M was used in our sample) and paint the top side of the dubbed body (*e*). This tinting of the dubbed fur on top will show through the transparent Swannundaze that is wound on next.

Spiral the Swannundaze forward to the thread. Tie it down securely, and snip off the excess (*f,g*).

Wind the string of black Monocord forward, in between the grooves of the Swannundaze. Secure the Monocord and snip off the excess (*h*).

Spin some of the prepared dubbing blend onto your thread and wind it around the hook shank all the way to the eye of the hook. Build a full, well-formed thorax (*i*). The thorax should be just slightly heavier than the abdomen. The last few windings of dubbing should terminate about one-sixteenth of an inch behind the eye of the hook. The thread should be left hanging directly on (not past) the forward part of the thorax area (*j*).

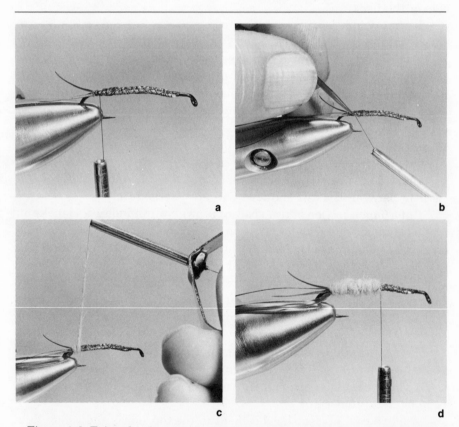

Figure 4–8. Tying the *Acroneuria*. (*a*) Tying in goose biots for tail. (*b*) Tying in Swannundaze. (*c*) Winding dubbing onto shank. (*d*) Dubbing wound over underbody material.

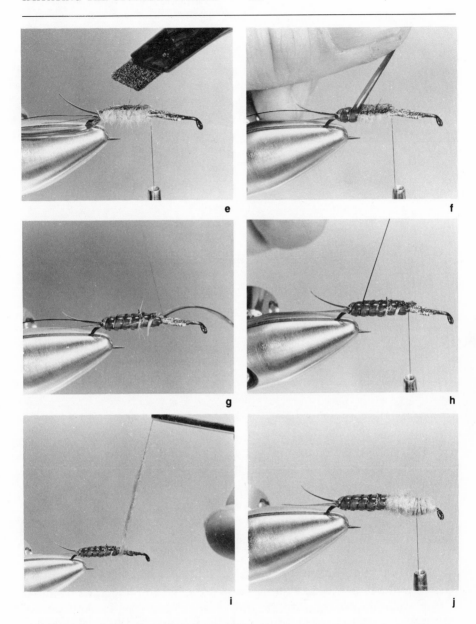

Figure 4–8 (continued). (e) Marking top of dubbed fur with brown Pantone. (f) Winding Swannundaze forward toward thread. (g) Completed abdomen. (h) Winding black Monocord rib through Swannundaze. (i) Winding dubbing for thorax. (j) Completed thorax.

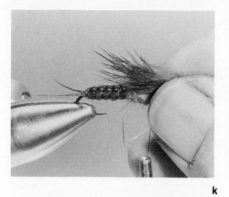

k

l

Figure 4–8 (continued). (*k*) Measuring mink fur for wing case. (*l*) Tying in wing case of mink fur. (*m*) Completed *Acroneuria*.

m

Cut a small bunch of mink (or similar) fur, about the diameter of a wooden matchstick, from the skin. If the bunch seems too bulky, remove some of the underfur. Be sure, however, not to disarrange the guard hairs from the bunch while you are removing underfur. Place the bunch on top of the hook shank so that the underfur covers the full thorax area and the hair fibers protrude beyond the thorax, toward the bend of the hook (*k,l*).

Now cut two smaller bunches of fur and tie one in on each side of the first bundle that you tied on. Be sure to leave the underside exposed. Apply some head lacquer to the thorax area where the fur is to be tied in. Mink fur fibers, especially, are extremely slippery. When the bunches have been securely fastened to the shank, snip off the excess fur and smooth out the area near the eye with turns of thread. Put a dab of clear lacquer on the thread windings. Because the wing case has been made of fur and hair, there is now no need to add legs.

Tie off the head, apply a touch of head lacquer, and let dry. The nymph is ready, but if you wish to add eyes, dab on black lacquer with a small dowel.

Inverted Acroneuria You can also tie the *Acroneuria* nymph so that it is inverted. In other words, you can tie it upside down, so that the hook point rides up. This is important, since most anglers agree that nymphs should be fished on the bottom. In fact, it's said that if you don't get hung up, or lose an imitation now and then, you are not fishing it properly.

The idea of the inverted nymph is not new. Jack Atherton dealt with the weighted, inverted Collins nymph in *The Fly and the Fish*. What makes the inverted nymph ideally suitable here is that we are using a fur thorax: Because the loosely tied fur is lighter than the hook and body of the fly, and because mink fur has the ability to float, the fur thorax will always ride above the hook shank even though submerged. It behaves somewhat like a parachute, staying above while the heavier hook shank hangs below. Thus the nymph rides as designed, upright yet inverted, with a hook point that is less likely to snag on rocks and logs.

When tying an inverted nymph, begin with the hook in an upright position in the vise. If you want your imitation to have a slight curve, bend the hook shank in the opposite direction.

Tie in the tail fibers and secure them. Now remove the hook from the vise and reinsert it in an upside-down position. Proceed with the construction of the nymph as before. You may find it a little difficult working around the hook point, but patience and a little finger licking can com-

Figure 4–9. Inverted *Acroneuria*.

plete the job. Figure 4–9 shows the completed fly. Does it not open up other areas of speculation?

Acroneuria with Standard Wing Case This time we are going to show you how Bill Simpson of Newtown, Connecticut, ties his *Acroneuria*. A professional tyer, Bill had to devise a quicker way to turn out his stonefly nymphs without sacrificing effectiveness.

BILL SIMPSON'S ACRONEURIA (Figure 4–10)

HOOK SIZE: 6 to 12 (Mustad #9575)

THREAD: Dark brown

TAIL: Two brown goose biots

UNDERBODY: Plastic form over which yellow dubbing is wound the length of the abdomen

ABDOMEN: Transparent brown Swannundaze material

THORAX: Pale amber dubbing

WING CASE: Ringneck pheasant body feathers (or suitable substitute) burned to shape

LEGS: Speckled hen saddle or wood duck flank fibers

ANTENNAE: Fox whiskers

When Bill begins the construction of this pattern (the hook used here is a size 8), he first ties in the plastic form, which is lashed to the shank by liberal turns of thread and coated with Krazy Glue (*a*).

Bill then forms a small ball with dubbing fur at the bend of the hook, and ties in the goose fiber tails (*b,c*). The small fur ball allows Bill to get instant outward flare of the tail fibers without spending time manipulating them.

The Swannundaze material is tied in next (*d*). Notice that Bill uses no ribbing material; that's because he later forms the segments by winding the Swannundaze in slightly open spirals across the underbody of fur.

He then winds the dubbing fur over the plastic form until the thread is left hanging at a point three-fifths of the distance forward of the hook bend (*e*). The Swannundaze material is now wound in an open spiral to the thread and secured (*f, g*).

After this, Bill spins some pale amber dubbing fur onto the thread to build one-third of the thorax area.

A half dozen fibers from a speckled light brown hen saddle feather, or wood duck flank feather, are tied in on the far side of the thorax (*h*).

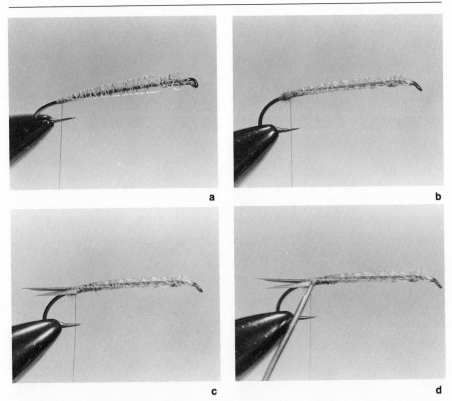

Figure 4–10. Tying Bill Simpson's *Acroneuria*. (*a*) Tying plastic form to shank. (*b*) Tying in ball of dubbing at bend of hook. (*c*) Tying in goose biot tails. (*d*) Tying in Swannundaze.

The fibers form the legs and should extend rearward and outward at an angle for half an inch. By tying the fibers into the fur thorax, Bill gets them to flare easily. He then does the same to the other side, and winds a bit more fur to fill in the area just behind the point where the fibers were tied in.

Bill then ties in a preshaped ringneck body feather, a "church-window" from a male pheasant. He always preshapes and prepares a number of these feathers before any tying session, in order to save time. The feathers are dipped into a bottle of Ambroid cement and allowed to dry, after which they are put in a wing burner. After burning, Bill uses a dubbing needle or the blunt edge of a pair of scissors to scrape away any burnt residue still protruding from the edge of the wing burner.

In the next step, the wing case is tied in just forward of the legs, so

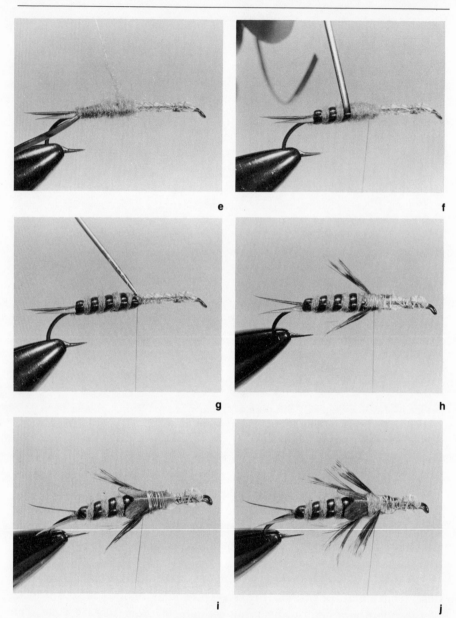

Figure 4–10 (continued). (*e*) Winding dubbing fur over plastic body. (*f*) Winding Swannundaze forward. (*g*) Tying down Swannundaze. (*h*) Tying first set of hen fibers for legs. (*i*) Tying in first wing case. (*j*) Tying in second set of legs.

that it extends rearward as shown (*i*). More Ambroid cement on top of the wing case makes it lie flat.

Bill spins more dubbing onto his thread and winds it over the butts of the wing case; he then ties in two more sets of fiber legs, one on each side of the shank (*j*).

Bill then ties in another prepared wing case, the same size as the first, at a point slightly more than one-eighth of an inch forward of the first. He cements the top of the second wing case and adds dubbing fur over the base.

Next, the last set of legs is tied in, one on each side of the hook shank. When Bill ties in the last set, his thread is just over the little "V" notch in the plastic underbody (*k*), He secures the legs in this notch and cements it.

The whiskers of an animal such as the fox, opossum, or mink are used for the antennae, being tied in in so that the tips extend outward at an angle, and extend approximately a quarter-inch past the eye of the hook (*l*).

Bill prepares the foundation for the pronotum with a little more dubbing, so that the remainder of the shank is completely filled to the eye. He has his own wing burner for the pronotum, but you can shape it as shown with scissors. Cut it almost square (with a very slight indent) at the end of the feather. Bill ties the pronotum feather in on top of the hook shank, slightly more than one-eighth inch forward of the last wing case *(m)*.

k   l

Figure 4–10 (continued). (*k*) Tying in second wing case and third set of legs. (*l*) Tying in animal whiskers as feelers.

Figure 4–10 (continued). (*m*) Tying in pronotum feather. (*n*) Bill Simpson's completed *Acroneuria*.

He then snips away the excess butt, cements the top of the pronotum, covers any exposed fluff with turns of thread, and then whip finishes and touches off the windings with cement. The eyes, which are optional, are painted on the head (*n*).

Brooks' Montana Stone

One of the most effective, sensible, and easiest nymphs to tie is Charles Brooks' Montana Stone, his version of *Pteronarcys californica*. We had the privilege of fishing with Charlie in July of 1979 and watching him tie. He likes his nymphs tied "in the round" for fast water. Then, no matter which way the current tosses the nymph, it looks okay to the fish because the "correct" side is always up.

BROOKS' MONTANA STONE

HOOK SIZE: 4, 4XL
THREAD: Black
TAIL: Six fibers from a raven or crow primary feather, tied forked
UNDERBODY: Twenty-five turns of .025-inch lead wire
BODY: Black yarn or fur
RIBBING: Oval copper tinsel
HACKLE: One grizzly hackle, one brown-dyed grizzly hackle, and
    two strands of gray ostrich herl

Charlie first ties on the tails (3 fibers on each side) so they are forked. Next, he ties in the ribbing and black fuzzy yarn. He then weights the hook with 25 turns of lead wire. The yarn is then wound forward to the eye, then back to just short of the bend, forward to the eye again, and then back one-third the length of the body. Here the yarn is tied off.

After tying off the yarn, Charlie spirals the ribbing forward to the point at which he tied off the yarn and ties off the ribbing at this same point. He then ties in both hackles and two strands of gray ostrich herl at the base of the thorax. After this, Charlie takes his one grizzly hackle and his one dyed-brown grizzly hackle and strips off the fibers on the lower edge of the hackle so that all the fibers are on one side. Both hackles are then wound one turn at the base of the thorax, spiraled forward one-quarter inch on the bottom, wound one more turn, and then tied off.

Completing the nymph, Charlie winds the ostrich herl over the base of the hackle windings and ties it off. He half-hitches the tying thread forward, and finishes the head.

The finished Montana Stone has one turn of hackle at the rear of the thorax and the other turn of hackle a quarter-inch forward. With just a little proper fishing technique, Charlie's round style works for other nymph imitations besides *Pteronarcys*.

Small Stonefly Nymphs

Many of the large stonefly patterns can be reduced in size and changed in color to imitate smaller nymphs, such as *Capnia, Nemoura,* and *Isoperla,* tied on size 10 or 12, or even 16 or 18 hooks. Better yet, you can simplify the patterns. Simple patterns can be very effective and, of course, are much easier to tie.

Here is a pattern for the small yellow nymph, *Isoperla bilineata.* Actually, it could be any *Isoperla* or even *Alloperla*. Strictly speaking, precise imitation of *Isoperla bilineata* probably should call for a quill abdomen, since nymphs of this species look hairless. Yet here we use fur dubbing because fur just makes the nymph seem more alive.

YELLOW STONEFLY

HOOK SIZE: 12 to 16 (Mustad #9671)
THREAD: Yellow
TAILS: Yellow goose short side quill fibers
ABDOMEN: Yellow fur

THORAX: Yellow fur
SEGMENTS: Yellow Monocord
WING CASE: Light mottled turkey (or similar feather) dyed yellow
LEGS: Soft yellow hen hackle

Tie in the tails, abdomen, and ribbing in the conventional manner. Upon reaching the thorax, tie in the wing case feather upside down and extend it rearward.

Tie in the hen hackle, which will represent the legs, on top of the wing case feather in an upside-down position.

Tie in the thorax, then let the thread hang behind the eye of the hook.

Pull the hen hackle feather tautly forward and secure it with tying thread. Pull the wing case feather forward, forcing the hen fibers downward to form the legs. Whip finish, lacquer the head, and clip off any excess material.

Small nymphs like the Yellow Stonefly are often weighted with strips of lead attached to the sides of the hook shank.

Instead of fur, wood duck, teal, or mallard flank feathers can be used for the abdomen and thorax. In fact, you can tie the whole nymph from a single feather. Here's how to tie *I. bilineata* using mallard feathers dyed yellow.

ONE-FEATHER NYMPH (Figure 4–11)

HOOK SIZE: 12 to 16 (Mustad #9671)
THREAD: Flymaster dark brown
TAILS: Six fibers from mallard flank feather dyed yellow
RIBBING: Fine gold oval tinsel
ABDOMEN: Yellow mallard feathers spiraled around hook
WING CASE: Yellow mallard fibers
THORAX: Yellow mallard fluff

Bend the hook, place it in the vise, and tie in the tail (*a-d*). Tie in the ribbing (*e*). Tie in the mallard fibers and wrap them around the shank forward to the bend of the hook (*f,g*). Be sure to taper the abdomen. Spiral the ribbing forward over the abdomen (*h*). Tie in the wing case at the rear end (*i*). Dub the fluff for the thorax (*j,k*). Bring the wing case feathers forward over the top of the thorax and tie them down (*l*). Divide the tapered fibers left over from the wing case with figure-eights of the turning thread so that they extend backwards as legs (*m,n*). Whip finish the head.

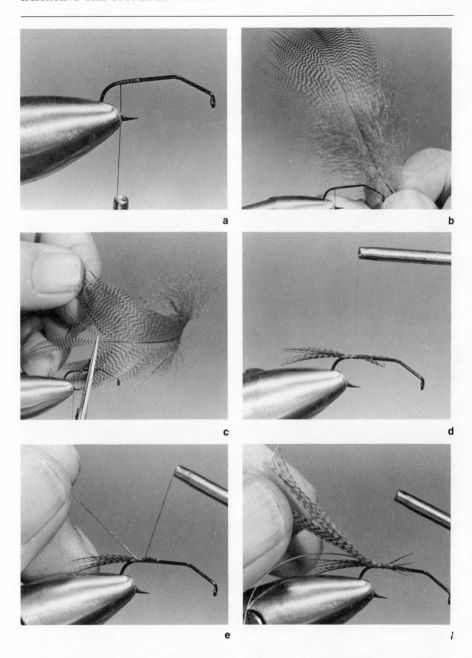

Figure 4–11. Tying the One-Feather Nymph. (*a*) Bending hook to shape. (*b*) Mallard flank feather dyed yellow. (*c*) Cutting section of fibers for tail. (*d*) Tying in tail. (*e*) Tying in ribbing. (*f*) Tying in mallard feathers for body.

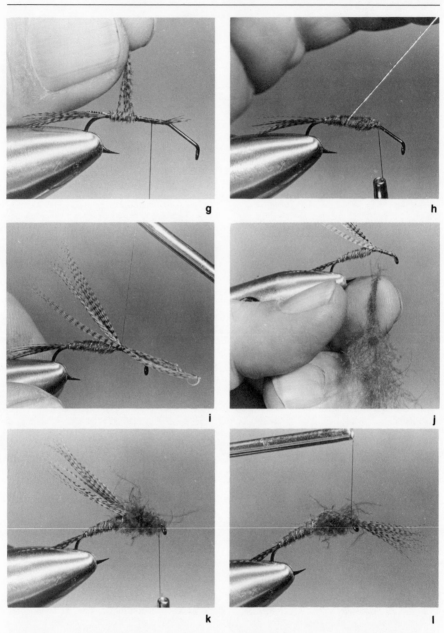

Figure 4–11 (continued). (*g*) Winding mallard fibers around hook shank. (*h*) Spiraling ribbing forward over abdomen. (*i*) Tying in mallard fibers for wing case. (*j*) Dubbing mallard fluff to thread. (*k*) Winding dubbed mallard fluff for thorax. (*l*) Mallard fibers brought forward and tied down to form wing case.

Figure 4–11 (continued). (*m*) Dividing mallard fibers with figure-eights of turning thread. (*n*) Forcing mallard fibers down and rearward to form legs. (*o*) One-Feather Nymph complete.

It goes without saying, but we'll say anyway, that you can use any feather with fibers of sufficient length to imitate any nymph, be it a stonefly or a mayfly.

Last but not least, the pattern descriptions for the Woolly Worms read as follows:

BLACK WOOLLY WORM (Figure 4–12)

HOOK SIZE: 2 to 12 (Mustad #38941 or #79580)
THREAD: Black
TAIL: Red hackle fibers
BODY: Black chenille
RIB: Flat silver tinsel
HACKLE: Grizzly palmered through body

Figure 4–12. Black Woolly Worm.   Figure 4–13. Black Woolly Bug.

BROWN WOOLLY WORM

HOOK SIZE: 2 to 12 (Mustad #38941 or #79580)
THREAD: Black
TAIL: Red hackle fibers
BODY: Brown chenille
RIB: None
HACKLE: Grizzly palmered through body

Woolly Worms are among the flies easiest to tie. In the case of the Black Woolly Worm, the red tail is tied in first in such a way that it extends about one-quarter inch past the bend.

Next, a grizzly hackle feather is tied in by its tip, over the tail butts at the bend. The tinsel ribbing is then tied in. A 5- to 6-inch rope of chenille is de-cored at one end, and the thread cores are tied to the hook shank at the bend. The size of the chenille to be used depends on the hook; generally, a size 3 chenille is used for hooks of sizes 2 and 4, a size 2 chenille is used for hooks of sizes 6 and 8, and a size 1 chenille is used for size 10 and 12 hooks.

The Woolly Worm can also be tied in a weighted version. If this is to be done, the simple method of wrapping spirals of lead wire around the hook shank, overwinding with thread, and then lacquering with cement is the proper procedure.

After the lacquering step, the thread is brought to a position just before the eye of the hook, and the chenille is wound to the same position in closely connecting spirals. When the chenille has reached the thread, it is tied down with it.

The tinsel is now wound forward in an open spiral to the thread and tied down.

Last, the grizzly hackle feather is wound through the chenille, in an open spiral between the tinsel windings, to the thread. All excesses are trimmed, the fly is finished off with a whip-finish knot and lacquer is applied to the windings.

In the same family as the Woolly Worm is another scraggly fly called, variably, the Cape Cod Woolly, the Woolly Bear, and also the Black Woolly Bug. This fly resembles something of a cross between a Woolly Worm and a Leech Fly. The best that can be said about it is that it is ugly. When fished, however, it is called beautiful. Like the Woolly Worm, the Cape Cod Woolly is often taken for a stonefly nymph, and probably for everything else. It works well not only on the bottom but also just beneath the surface. It is also very easy to tie. You can't tie it improperly, and many tyers use only the dregs of their tying materials for this pattern, which is made of the following components:

BLACK WOOLLY BUG (Figure 4–13)

> HOOK SIZE: 2 to 12 (Mustad #38941 or #79580)
> THREAD: Black
> TAIL: Black hen hackle fibers or black marabou
> BODY: Black wool, fur, or peacock herl
> RIB: Black hackle palmered through body
> HACKLE: Black hen hackle tied as collar

The procedures for tying this pattern are the same as for the standard Woolly Worm. The fly can be tied either unweighted or weighted.

FISHING THE
STONEFLY NYMPH

When fishing with nymphs in any rapids, I consider
my stonefly nymphs the most necessary of all.
The trout eat all they can seize.

—Sid Gordon, *How to Fish from Top to Bottom*

NYMPH FISHING IS LIKE worm fishing. Anyone who can take trout with
worms can do so with a nymph. Heretical statements? No, the truth. Both
call for bottom fishing. But let us quickly point out that not everyone can
take trout readily with worms. There is as much difference between a
successful worm fisherman and a fisherman who uses worms as there is
between a practiced nymph fisherman and a fisherman who uses nymphs.

Like a successful worm fisherman, a good nymph fisherman has developed and refined his bottom techniques, and has added a few extra
wrinkles through observation and experience. He'll know from turning
over rocks that the larger stoneflies, such as the Perlidae and Pteronarcyidae, are more to be found under and around large rocks in a fast
current than in a slow run with a weedy bottom. He'll also know that a
little roach-like creature, *Peltoperla,* is to be found in abundance in the
packets of dead leaves that have collected around a submerged log, and
that those green, yellow, or light brown little nymphs, the Chloroperlidae,

prefer mixed gravel where they can crawl through the bottom sediments. In brief, the successful fisherman, from his choice of tackle to his choice of nymph, is systematic. He knows what he's doing and why, while the less successful angler relies on chuck, chance, and a prayer.

There are different ways to fish the nymph successfully. That's because different methods are required for different waters. You adapt your method to the water. For example, Chuck Fothergill, as we shall see, uses a weighted 15-foot leader with his floating line out of the water, while Charles Brooks uses a sinking-tip line and a leader never more than 6 feet long. Both are successful. Why? Because their methods are adapted to the type of water they fish. Brooks fishes in very fast runs 5 or 6 feet deep; Fothergill fishes deep pocket water studded with huge boulders. If they changed places, they would have to change techniques. Both want the nymph on the bottom.

The Rod

The right tackle is essential for successful nymph fishing. The rod should be long, 9 feet or more. A long rod gives you more control than a short rod in mending line. A long rod also enables you to reach out farther and —important point—it enables you to keep a straight line for detection of a hesitation, a pause, or a check in the progress of the line that may indicate a take. Say you're fishing a run. In the normal course of events and if all goes well, a trout on station, sampling the tidbits that come its way, will spot the nymph coming downstream along the bottom. The fish has no need to expend energy with violent movement at this time. Nature will provide. Along comes a natural nymph. The trout takes it by cavitation. It simply opens its mouth to create a space which water, carrying the nymph, fills. "Yum, yum," thinks the trout of the natural, and down goes the nymph. Now along comes your nymph. The trout opens its mouth. Water rushes in. The trout closes its mouth. "Yech," thinks the trout, and ejects the nymph.

You have to pay attention or you won't catch fish. The pause, the hesitation, the check in your line occur while the nymph is in the trout's mouth and before the fish goes "yech." And that's the time you have to strike. This is not to imply that there won't be times when you get a hard strike, but the pause takes are common when fishing the nymph. Sometimes you may not even notice the line hesitate, but you'll see what Skues called "the wink" as the trout opens its mouth.

Inasmuch as you're going to be fishing stonefly nymphs, some of them weighted, some perhaps tied on a size 2 or 4 hook, you'll want to be able to put a nymph where you want. With a 9-foot rod, a 6 or 7 line is the most practical choice.

What kind of action should the rod have? Years ago it used to be thought that a limber rod, or one with slow action, was best for nymphs. The idea was that if a trout took your imitation, the slow movement of the rod tip would allow for some give and take and not break off the fish. However, when a nymph is fished properly, a limber rod does not respond quickly enough to allow you to set the hook between the time the line pauses and the fish ejects the nymph. A compromise is in order. The rod action should be in the medium range, neither too fast nor too slow.

Graphite, glass, or bamboo? Of the three, the graphite rod is the fastest. However, the longer the graphite rod, the greater the flex. If you choose graphite you need at least a 9½-foot rod to give you the desired action. Glass has more flex, and here a 9-foot rod will do. Bear in mind that we're generalizing, since taper, which also relates to line weight, is also involved. Bamboo is very similar to glass in action, although it recovers much more quickly. Many anglers prefer a fine bamboo because it is a lovely thing to behold. But a word of advice. Pick and choose carefully when you buy a bamboo rod; because they are made from a natural fiber, no two are alike even though they come from the same manufacturer, have the same height and taper, and are designated for the same line weight. Be particular. If you do find that "one in a rack" it will be a joy forever; or at least until you slam a car door on it.

Reels

The reel should match the rod for balance. Ideally, a rod and reel is in balance when the point at which you grip the rod becomes the fulcrum with 30 feet of line out of the rod tip. A well-manufactured single-action reel capable of holding your line and backing comfortably is what you want.

Lines

There is much confusion among anglers today about which line to use, especially since manufacturers make a special model for nearly every conceivable stream, lake, or ocean fishing situation. One manufacturer lists no fewer than 25 different types of lines, each having its own particular use. All of these varieties are broken down into weight designations ranging from a number 1 level line to a number 15 shooting taper.

For fishing stonefly imitations, we need only be concerned with a few fly-fishing lines, primarily the full-floating and the sink-tip variety. Lines are usually designated with code letters and numbers; for example, a number 6 weight-forward floating line will be designated as WF-6-F. The first code, WF, indicates the type of taper, in this case a weight-forward. The second code, or 6, gives us the line weight (approximately 160 grains for the first 30 feet). The last code, F, tells us that the line will float.

If a line is intended to sink it is designated with an S. For example, if our WF-6-F were a sinking line it would have been labeled WF-6-S. In addition to the available conventional floating and sinking lines, most manufacturers today make lines that are a combination of the two; these are called floating/sinking lines, or floating lines with sink tips. A WF-6 line similar to those above would then be designated as WF-6-F/S. These floating/sinking lines are further broken down into the number of feet of the foreportion of the line that consist of sinking material. For example, Scientific Angler makes three different sink-tip lines; one is called a Wet Tip F/S, on which the first 10 feet of the line sink while the remainder floats. Another, the Wet Belly, has 20 feet of sinking line; while yet another, the Wet Head, features 30 feet of sinking line before the floating portion begins. All of the sink-tip lines are two-tone; in other words, the sinking portion is of one color while the floating part is another color (usually the sinking portion is the darker of the two colors).

For much of our stonefly fishing a conventional floating line is used. It is only when we get into deeper and faster water that the sink-tip lines are employed. In extreme cases, such as occur in some of the Far Western deep-cut and fast-flowing steelhead streams, an experienced angler will use a fast-sinking shooting-head line backed with monofilament running line. The line is cast upstream for distances of 70 feet and more, so that it has a chance to sink all the way to the stream bed. In some cases the anglers using this technique are fishing in water over 12 feet deep that is rushing downgrade very rapidly.

A shooting-head line is only 30 feet long. When you are ready to cast, the entire line protrudes beyond the tip of the rod by only 3 to 4 inches. Monofilament is used as a backing because it slips through the guides extremely well after it has been properly stretched, giving the line length and depth needed for the fast, deep steelhead water. (When coiled on a reel or spool, monofilament develops "memory" coils; in order to take the coils out, an angler will pull the monofilament through his hands slowly, but tautly. Another method is to have two anglers, one at each end of a 70- or 80-foot stretch of line, pulling steadily on the monofilament but not strongly enough to break it.)

Fishing a stonefly nymph with a shooting-head sinking line is the most difficult of all methods, since it is almost impossible to detect a "take" by a trout. There is also no way in which you can mend a shooting-head line with 50 or more feet of running line backing up your cast. All you can do in such a situation is to bring in any slack line that piles back on you after you make your upstream cast. When you see the line hesitate in the stream current as it is tumbling down on you . . . strike! That hesitation may be a trout that has intercepted your nymph. In some instances you may even see the line moving perceptibly back upstream as a trout begins to return to his station.

Mending

Mending a fly line after it has been cast is an important part of every angler's fishing technique, whether for dry- or wet-fly fishing. The purpose of mending a line is to allow the fly to float downsteam without drag; it is actually used more with a floating line than with a sinker. Casting a sink-tip line while quartering upstream presents some problems in line mending. A floating fly line cast either directly across or quartering upstream will generally be pushed by a current stronger than that in which

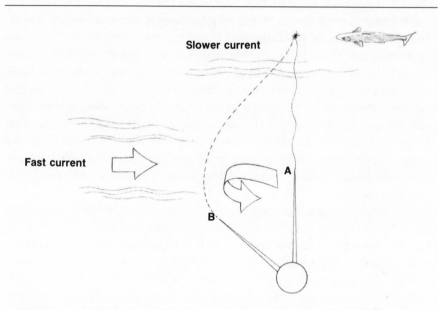

Figure 5–1. Mending line when casting across a stream or quartering upstream.

the angler is standing or the fly is floating; the line will therefore drift downstream faster than the fly. The fly line then forms a "belly" in the stream, dragging the fly with it—unnaturally. In order to overcome this drag problem the angler should point the rod tip toward the line as it floats on the water, and with a deft motion swing the tip upward in an arc toward the upstream direction from which the current is coming. If done with proper force this will lift much of the line from the water and re-form it in a curve upstream from the fly (Figure 5–1). It will then take a little while before the stronger, middle current of the stream again pushes the fly line down far enough to drag the fly.

However, when fishing accurately to a particular rising fish, the preceding method of mending line on the water leaves something to be desired, simply because when making the mend, you are also pulling the fly out of position. When you want to pinpoint your cast you will do better by making what is known as an upstream hold cast. This cast is somewhat like mending a line before it comes into contact with the water. To accomplish this maneuver you must first spool 6 or 7 feet of extra line from your reel and allow it to lie loosely by your side in the water. Then, as you make your forward cast, you first make sure, with a false cast or two, that your fly is over the target area (usually 3 or 4 feet upstream of where the fish is lying). After making your cast and while the fly is headed toward the target, bring the rod tip upstream on a horizontal plane above the water, while simultaneously releasing the line with your reel hand. The loose line at your side should then shoot through the guides of your rod (Figure 5–2). What happens in such a maneuver is that the line, with the fly and leader, and after having been cast forward, carries straight to your target; only the excess 6 or 7 feet that came off your reel is absorbed through the guides as you bring your rod tip upstream. You will thus have your line well upstream, with the fly just above the lie of the trout, allowing you plenty of time and room for a drag-free float. The upstream hold cast can also be used with sinking lines, but this usually requires additional conventional mending.

The secret in mending a sinking or sink-tip line is to do your mending the moment the line touches the water. At that moment, you can get a loop upstream and give the leader and fly a head start downstream. Once the sinking or sink-tip line has penetrated the surface, you will not be able to mend. The easiest sinking line to mend, of course, is the Wet Tip with its short 10-foot sink tip. After the initial surface-touching mend, this line can be mended in its floating portion, yielding a fairly full, drag-free float with the fly on the bottom.

In stonefly nymph fishing, the depth and speed of the water current

PLATE 1

Catskill Curler
(Vinciguerra)

Pteronarcys Californica Nymph
(McNeese)

K's Butt Salmonfly
(Boyle)

Don's Brown Stonefly Nymph
(Neve and Fox)

Giant Black Nature Nymph
(Mathews)

Curved Dorsata Nymph
(Neve and Fox)

PLATE 2

K's Butt Stonefly
(Boyle)

Henwing Bomber
(Neve and Fox)

Little Black Stonefly Dry
(Neve and Fox)

Pteronarcys Californica Adult
(McNeese)

Calineuria Californica Adult
(McNeese)

Polar Commander
(Neve and Fox)

Hair Wing Stonefly
(Borger)

PLATE 3

Claassenia Nymph
(Quammen)

Mono Stonefly Nymph
(Borger)

Calineuria Californica Nymph
(McNeese)

Hesperoperla Pacifica Nymph
(McNeese)

Don's Mottled Stonefly Nymph
(Neve and Fox)

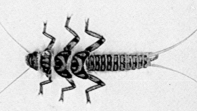

Ultra-Realistic Acroneuria
(Schmookler)

Curved
Lycorias Nymph
(Neve and Fox)

Delaware Yellow Stonefly Wet
(Vinciguerra)

Monty's Golden Stone
(Montplaisir)

PLATE 4

Early Brown Stonefly Wet
(Vinciguerra)

Isoperla Fulva Nymph
(McNeese)

Red Brown Nymph
(Borger)

Poly-Caddis Style Fly, Capniidae
(Borger)

Little Black Stonefly Nymph
(Neve and Fox)

Peltoperla Nymph
(Schmookler)

Needlefly
(McNeese)

Taeniopteryx Nymph
(McNeese)

Isoperla Fulva Adult
(McNeese)

Little Yellow Adult, with Egg Sac
(McNeese)

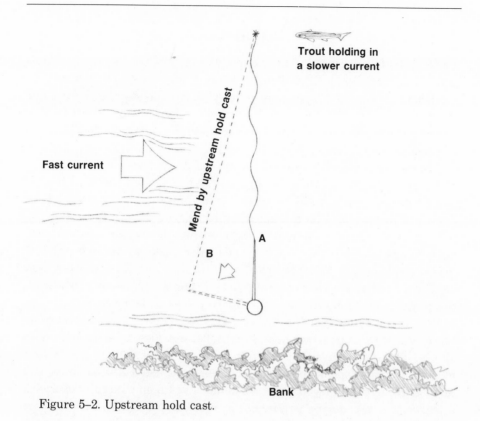

Figure 5–2. Upstream hold cast.

will dictate what kind of sinking line to use. In most average waters where the stream is no more than 4 feet deep, the conventional floating line, with a weighted nymph, can be fished successfully. In the deeper currents, a 10-foot sink-tip line will generally suffice. In the really deep fast-moving streams, a shooting-head line is preferable over the Wet Belly or Wet Head types of line.

Some lines made especially for nymph fishing have a bright color near the tip so that you can more easily detect a pause or a take. Also on the market is a "Strike Indicator," manufactured by Cortland; this is a piece of fluorescent plastic that you attach to your line behind the leader. When, some years ago, Dave Whitlock was lecturing at the Federation of Fly Fishermen's Conclave in Sun Valley, Idaho, and recommended that the line and leader be connected with a piece of bright fluorescent fly line, someone in the audience shouted, "Why don't you use a bobber?" Dave answered, "It won't fit through the guides."

Leaders

The length of leader you will need depends on where you're fishing. Water depth and current velocities play key roles. If you're using a floating line, the leader should be long enough to let your nymph stay on the bottom. Generally, leaders for a floating line range in length from 10 to 18 feet. There are a number of chemically based products on the market that you can apply to your leader to get it to sink.

Since many stonefly nymphs are of medium to large size, a 3X tippet will generally suffice, although there may be times when you want to drop to a 4X or move up to a 2X. The size of your imitation and the size of the trout you're after will be the determining factors.

As we noted above—and we cannot stress this enough—water conditions will dictate your choice of line and leader. In deep water a 5- or 6-foot leader attached to a fast-sinking or sink-tip line will get you down very well, and you can actually control it better than a long leader. To a trout, the leader and the fly line are only more pieces of debris in the stream, so long as the nymph acts naturally. Lefty Kreh often uses a leader of no more than 18 inches when fishing nymphs, wet flies, or streamers on a sinking line. Lefty says, "I don't use it in tiny brooks where the impact of the line might spook the fish, but otherwise I use it all the time. You have more control and you get down faster. I've taken wild rainbows with a leader so short, maybe two inches at most, that I couldn't tie another knot in it."

Another reason for using a short leader on sinking or sink-tip lines is that it will stay closer to the bottom than a long leader. For example, a 12-foot leader in moving water may actually ride higher than the fly line itself as the drift is made downstream.

Casting

Casting a nymph, particularly a large and weighted one, doesn't call for all the elegance and grace you may have learned at the fly-fishing school or clinic, and polished in your back yard. In fact, some die-hard nymph fishermen have almost forgotten how to cast a dry fly. Instead of casting with a tight loop, they lob the nymph; they have to because of the weight involved. But although nymph fishing has none of the elegance and grace of dry-fly fishing, it demands concentration. You must keep an intent watch on your line for any checks or pauses that might indicate a take. More often than not, that hesitation means a snag, but you still have to strike quickly, since it might be a fish. Then again, you may be startled by a sudden hard strike. This constant concentration can be tiring, but the results can be very rewarding.

Emerging Nymphs

It's an experienced fisherman who will take advantage of emerging nymphs. But you'd be cutting your chances of success by tying on an Early Brown in May, when that species has already been long gone. Sure a fish could take it for some other species, but you're a step ahead of the game if you know that *Acroneuria carolinensis* or *Allonarcys biloba* or whatever are about to emerge. You can find out by looking for the nymphal skin cases or shucks on the shore and on rocks above the water. You can also check the emergence tables in the Appendix. Granted, more research has to be done nationally to pinpoint the emergence periods of many stonefly species on many streams, but the tables will give you some glimmer of what's on the move toward shore at what time of year. Dr. Richard J. Neves, who spent three years studying the seasonal succession and diversity of stoneflies in a Massachusetts stream—his emergence table for Factory Brook appears in the Appendix—advises that "since emergence occurs early in the morning or at dusk, fishermen have the best success using . . . imitations at these times. Nymphs are fished slowly along the bottom, particularly near streambanks or boulders projecting out of the water. These are the most likely sites for nymphs to crawl out of the stream, and where trout usually wait for prey." Neves warns that trout feeding on emerging nymphs "frequently strike hard, since the nymphs can cling securely to objects with their powerful legs and claws. Fly fishermen accustomed to the 'slurp' feeding of trout on surface flies are frequently caught off guard by the first strike at their nymph."

Behavioral Drift

As much as you might take advantage of emerging nymphs, use behavioral drift to your advantage. Numerous studies show that the best time for fishing a nymph is at dusk and during the first three hours after sunset. If you want to catch fish—and they'll most likely be small—don't bother with a stonefly nymph; instead, tie on a *Baetis* mayfly nymph or a scud. But if you want a chance at big trout, try a big stonefly nymph. Trout choose stations that are best suited to intercept drift, and they defend their territories, where they "positively select" the largest prey. Dr. Thomas F. Waters of the University of Minnesota, an ardent fly fisherman as well as a leading authority on drift, told us that "big trout do drift feed to a great extent. The best trout in the system will get the best feeding situation. That's where the water is coming in with the greatest collecting ability, such as the head of a pool where the water comes off riffles."

Although scientists did not know of behavioral drift until publication of the papers by Tanaka, Waters, and Müller in the early 1960s (see chapter 2), it is worth noting that almost half a century ago, Edward R. Hewitt was aware of something happening on trout waters as darkness fell, although few fishermen paid Hewitt any heed. In an article published in the March 1933 issue of *Field & Stream,* and which Hewitt reprinted in 1934 in his booklet *Nymph Fly Fishing,* he wrote:

The May-fly nymphs are very likely to come out and swim in the water toward dark, and they all [mayflies, stoneflies, and caddis] move about after dark. That is one reason why late fishing is so effective; trout do most of their feeding at this time. Nymphs are vastly better than surface flies after dark. In fact, I have often seen the water alive with trout moving at dark and have been able to get very few rises on a dry fly at such a time, when a nymph fly of the right pattern and size would take trout as fast as wanted. The latter represented the type of food the trout were feeding on.

Last season gave me many instances of the great superiority of this kind of fishing over the dry fly. On one occasion I fished one of my large pools with two separate dry flies as carefully as I knew how. A friend had just fished the pool ahead of me with another dry fly. The net result of both our efforts was one trout and two rises.

I then put on one of my stone-fly nymphs tied on a No. 14 hook and began at the top of the pool, fishing downstream. Only a few casts were made before I had a trout. Standing in the same place without moving down, I took fifteen fish and did not bother to fish the rest of the pool, as I was getting them too fast for pleasure. Some of the fish were of good size, and none of these were seen with the dry fly.

Hewitt was the father of nymph fishing in the United States. He has been dead for 25 years, but let's see what those who have followed in the field have done.

R. "Monty" Montplaisir lives in a trailer in Colebrook, New Hampshire, near the Canadian border. He ties flies for a living. He is 35 years old, and has been fishing since he was 6. From that description you might think Monty was some rustic out in the boonies. He is, but by choice. He is so smitten with fishing that he gave up his job as a fashion buyer for a Boston department store several years ago so he could fish and hunt full time. He fishes the headwaters of the Connecticut River, and he is an enthusiast of big stonefly nymphs. His Golden Stone pattern is given in chapter 8.

Monty uses an 8-foot graphite rod with a number 6 floating line. His leaders are long, 15 to 20 feet, and he fishes them with a short floating line of 6 to 15 feet. He fishes his stonefly nymphs in stretches where swift riffles empty into slower pools. Before he casts, he scouts the water to determine the possible holding position of the fish. He then slowly approaches the position from downstream. He gets as close as possible before he makes his cast. If the water is less than knee deep, he uses the weighted nymph. "My first cast is made upstream and well above the fish in the manner of a dry fly as I attempt a drag-free float," says Monty. "As the current brings the nymph back to me, I recover the excess line. I strike when I detect line hesitation or forward movement."

Should this approach fail, Monty changes his position so he can employ what he calls wet-fly technique. "I cast across the stream but well above the fish," he says. "As the nymph reaches the fish, I raise my rod tip slowly and give the fly line short quick strips. When the nymph swings below me, I lengthen the strips until the belly of the line has straightened in the current. Everything ceases at this point to about a count of two. I then jerk only the rod tip three or four times and take long strips of line in four or five times. Often the pause, quick jerk, and strip technique can

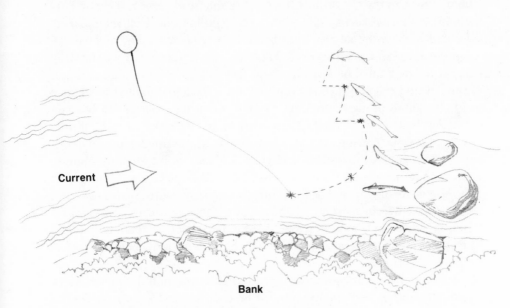

Figure 5–3. Monty Montplaisir's wet-fly technique.

be the difference between success and failure," explains Monty, whose wet-fly technique is shown in Figure 5–3. "I have watched browns leave their holding positions to follow a nymph downstream, and expected a response as the nymph turned in the current to straighten with the fly line. Instead these fish would take a position below the nymph and continue their inspection as it rose to the surface. The jerking of the rod tip would usually excite the fish and after a couple of quick strips the fish would take the nymph in a solid, slashing rise."

Should Monty need to get the nymph deeper to bounce the bottom, he uses a trick that Lefty Kreh taught him. When he ties on the nymph, he leaves about 2 or 3 inches of excess leader past the eye of the hook. He pinches a lead split shot—the size depends on the water depth—on the excess tippet, and singes the end with a cigarette so the split shot won't slide off.

Ted Niemeyer, who is a zealous and thoughtful student of aquatic entomolgy, is a stonefly enthusiast. He's fond of fishing big nymphs like *Pteronarcys* or *Allonarcys* very early in the morning. Most Eastern fishermen pass up the big nymph, and thereby miss out. You don't have to go West to find big nymphs. And *Allonarcys biloba* is every bit as big, if not bigger than, *Pteronarcys californica*.

Ted fishes in both the East and West. In the East he often fishes Esopus Creek in the Catskills. Like many a mountain creek, it has deeply cut banks where it turns and bends, and a shallow shore on the opposite side. Ted uses an 8-foot rod, number 6 line, 10-foot leader, and an unweighted Catskill Curler nymph. He carefully wades out from the deep side of the creek until he is about 3 feet from shore. Estimating the depth of the cut and the speed of the current, he affixes just enough lead wire to his leader to allow his nymph to drift along directly on the bottom. Counting the leader, he rarely has to cast or lob more than 30 feet of line.

By the time Ted enters the water, makes his estimates of the depth and current speed, affixes the lead wire, and ties on his stonefly nymph, enough time has elapsed for the creek to settle back to normal. As a fly tyer, Niemeyer never makes an unnecessary move with his thread, and he's the same way in a stream, doing no more false casting than necessary. When he figures it's time to move along, he goes downstream only a few feet at a time as he carefully probes the bottom with his boots so as not to alarm the trout.

His first lob is made almost directly upstream, and he immediately mends the line so that the nymph can find its way to the bottom. As the nymph progresses downstream, Ted mends his line again and again. If there is a pause in the line or leader, he strikes. In many instances, a snag

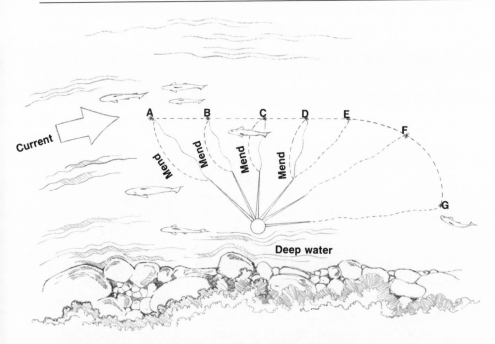

Figure 5–4. Ted Niemeyer's nymph-drifting technique.

will have caused the pause, but were he not to strike he might miss a fish.

As his nymph drifts downstream from where Niemeyer is standing, he has less and less need to mend line. Indeed, he may have to feed out a bit of line depending on the vagaries of the current. During the entire operation, which is shown in Figure 5–4, Ted holds the rod high to permit as much contact with the nymph as possible. He lets the nymph complete its swing at the end of the drift until it is directly downstream from him. Instead of picking up for another cast he lets it lift up in the current where, like Monty Montplaisir, he dances it in mid or top water. And as with Monty, the dancing imitation can invite a hard strike from a trout.

Ready for his next cast, Niemeyer will repeat the entire process. He moves downstream only when he's convinced that further casting in the same place would be unproductive. We have seen him take half a dozen good fish on an Eastern stream while most anglers fared poorly, and on the Big Wood River in Idaho, although outfished in quantity by others in the party, Niemeyer caught and released three big fish, including a 23½-inch rainbow that outweighed the total poundage of the trout caught by the other fishermen.

Fishing Runs and Pockets

When most of us see a big river for the first time—the Madison in Montana or the Ausable in New York—we're at a bit of a loss. Where does one begin to fish? There seems to be an endless flow of fast-moving, pocket-type water. Is it possible for a trout to be behind every depression, every boulder forming an eddy, or are the trout in the smooth glides between deflections? There are so many places that look good.

Unless you have a boat you can fish only the water that is accessible to you. Most stretches of the lower Madison are not practical for wading, and many anglers hire guides and float the river. On the other hand, New York's Ausable, while it does look menacing, is wadeable. When wading, it is a good idea to wear waders with sure-gripping felt soles or studs on the bottoms. A wading staff will also come in handy.

Runs and pocket water are fished in the same manner given for the shoreline technique. Since it's impractical to try to fish the entire river from shore to shore, you must concentrate on only that section of river that you can reach with your rod, line, and nymph.

Let's pretend that we have been taken to a brawling mountain stream that seems to be nothing more than one huge expanse of running water lined with pockets. Although the entire width of the river is wadeable, you should select a position a certain distance from shore and concentrate on the area that you can control. For example, if you're positioned 10 feet from shore, your casts should be made quartering upstream to your left and to your right, and your nymphs should float along the bottom in downstream lanes that are never farther than the length of your rod from your position. That's one of the reasons for a rod of 9 feet or more; it lets you cover more territory, while remaining in full control.

What you are doing is simply covering every inch of ground, beneath the water surface, that may hold a fish. After you have thoroughly covered the area around and some 30 feet below your position, take a few steps downstream and repeat the process. Again, as in the shoreline technique, don't reel in your nymph immediately at the end of the drift; instead, let it dance and weave in the water as it rides up. Incidentally, should a fish strike while your nymph is swinging on a downstream tight-line position, don't strike too hard. Better still, use a technique Lefty Kreh showed us and strike with a slack line. This is done by striking with the rod only; keep your hand away from the line.

When you have covered the water for a distance downstream and want to fish some of the middle water, or the water nearer to the other shore, get out of the river, walk back, and begin again, this time selecting another position in the stream. Then repeat the downstream process once more.

Long Rod, Long Leader

Another technique, which is especially useful in mountain streams with a lot of huge boulders, swirling eddies, and pocket water, is the long rod, long leader method. If you can imagine a long cane pole of some 10½ feet, to which an 18-foot leader has been tied you will get a good idea of what is going to happen. Generally, a goodly number of split shots is put about a foot above the nymph. The nymph is also weighted. The fly line itself rarely touches the water.

With the long rod and long leader you can swing the fly upstream, and by keeping the rod adjusted to the required distance, you have, in effect, a straight link to your nymph; there is no slack. The rod is moved downstream as fast as the current moves the nymph along the bottom. If there is a pause or hesitation indicating a take, the strike is made. This method is almost the only way to reach some of the trout lying in the swirling eddies behind boulders.

This is one technique used by Chuck Fothergill of Aspen, Colorado, when the situation calls for it.

Big Waters

Sometimes you really meet a river that is "too high, too wide, and too deep," and you can't get across to the other side, not even with a fly line. And yet in those deep glides there are rocks and boulders that spawn stoneflies and harbor trout. A lob cast won't reach these places, and even if it does, you don't have enough time or room to get your nymph to the bottom. Some of our Far Western states, and especially Alaska, have such rivers. And, if your travels should take you to such regions, you want to have every advantage. Rods of 9 feet or more are the rule on such waters, and line sizes of 8 and 9 are common because of the windy conditions most likely to prevail. You'll be using sink-tip lines under these conditions, with weighted flies and short leaders (usually no more than 5 feet). A 5-foot leader can be made by using the upper section of a tapered leader and measuring it down with a micrometer from .021 to .010—a length of about 3 feet—and then attaching 1 foot of .009 and 1 foot of .008, or approximately a 3X tippet. A lighter-test leader is made simply by jumping from .009 to .007, or a 4X tippet.

Your cast should be made quartering upstream, and should be mended as soon as the line touches the water. With a sink-tip line, this will be your only chance to mend the sinking portion at all. The floating portion can be mended again and again, as required. You want to get that nymph to the bottom as quickly as possible, and you want it to stay there as long as possible. As your line drifts and works its way downstream, pay close attention. Again, you must strike if there is any pause or hesitation in the line flow. And even though your casts be carefully and purposefully made, you will still find certain streams and stream situations that defy your best techniques.

When Angus Cameron, our editor, was in Alaska he found that the only way to get his imitation to the bottom was by making a long cast upstream and interrupting the cast as the rod tip passed twelve o'clock. When you interrupt a forward cast you do so by abruptly snubbing the rod tip after the power stroke has been applied; this makes the line jump back partially and form a number of S curves between the rod and the fly. The S's act as a buffer, or time delay, that permit a drag-free float before the line straightens out in the current. Figure 5–5 shows the technique. If, as the line is drifting down toward you, the S's begin to pause or move forward unnaturally . . . strike! You've got a fish (or maybe a snag). Still, even getting snagged on the bottom means you're fishing your fly properly.

There are also times when the all the mending and cast interrupting in the world doesn't work. It was under such circumstances that Ted Gerken, who runs the Iliaska Lodge in Iliamna, Alaska, said to Angus, "Let me show you a sourdough method for taking out the belly." Ted was referring to the curve in the line that was caused by the pressure of the current, and which the mending and interrupting of line didn't solve.

"Up here," Ted continued, "as the belly starts to develop, we simply wade downstream and thus prevent the belly from developing." For Angus, this method had to appear a bit unnatural, since he is a long-time, devout salmon fisherman. And, as only a salmon fisherman knows, you just don't walk downstream past a fish that may be lying there. "Well," said Ted, in reply to Angus's puzzlement, "up here we don't have to worry too much about casting to the same fish; there are many more to choose from." In addition to "walking" the line downstream, loose loops are also added if the angler cannot keep up with the drift of the fly.

Incidentally, you may have noticed that we didn't mention the name of the river in which the foregoing incident took place. That's because we don't know it. It happens to be an undisturbed river with a run of enormous rainbow trout. The trout take a number of years to reach their

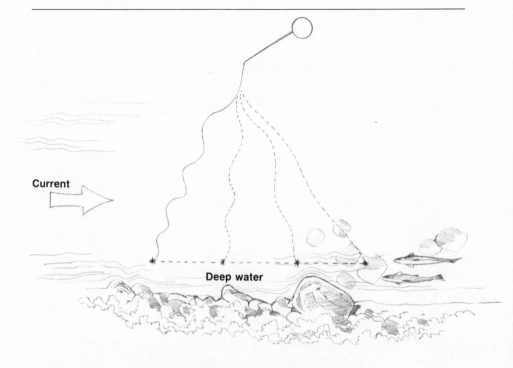

Figure 5–5. S curves for getting a nymph to the bottom.

average 7- to 15-pound size, and if we revealed the name of the river, Ted feels that it would be depleted very quickly. Except for one fish for mounting, Ted's clients release rainbows from this river.

Big waters can also be fished with a shooting-head sinking line backed with monofilament or level running line. In this case the cast is made very long, quartering upstream. Slack line is retrieved as the current pushes it back toward the angler. A belly will form on the sweep, and it is especially important to keep watch during this transition, since many fish strike on the sweep as the nymph comes off the bottom and begins to ride up.

Small Streams

When fishing a stonefly nymph on small streams (20 feet wide or less) with shallow depths, the method used for fishing dry flies can be used. The cast is made directly upstream using a floating line and a weighted nymph attached to a 9- or 10-foot leader. Since the line, leader, and fly will be coming directly back toward you in the same current lane, there is no variation as far as current speed is concerned, and thus no belly or drag occurs. However, you will have to keep taking in the loose coils of line as they move toward you. If there is a pause or hesitation in the line as it flows back toward you, by all means strike. The chances are your retrieval has been interupted by a trout or a snag.

In small streams there is no need for a sink-tip line, since most of the riffles and pockets will be only a foot or two deep. But don't let the size of the stream fool you as far as the size of the stoneflies that inhabit it go. If it's a fast-flowing and will-aerated piece of water, you're likely to reveal some fair-sized stonefly nymphs by turning over a few rocks. *Allonarcys* are often found in streams and brooks, and trout don't hesitate to make them their main meal.

Another method of fishing the small stream is to "walk the nymph" directly downstream. This is easily done by making a cast of line and leader straight downstream, interrupting the cast before it has been completed so that there is a bit of free-drifting slack line, and simply moving with the line as it moves downcurrent. However, a strike is difficult to detect with this method. What we usually do is to take a few steps downstream and pause, letting the line straighten and swing up from the bottom. It is during these pauses that the strike is felt. When a good fish strikes during such a pause, you can be broken off, since the fish will turn with the nymph to head back to his lie, while the force of your strike will pull the line in the opposite direction. You'll have to ease your strike or use the slack-line method of striking, that is, striking only with the rod hand as you let go of the line in your line hand.

Float Fishing

Many anglers prefer to fish the bigger waters from a boat. A good example of such big trout water is the Madison River in Montana. Though this river can be waded, there are certain spots and stretches of it, especially in high water, that can't be properly covered from a standing position in the stream. Outfitters such as Bob Jacklin and Bud Lilly of West Yellowstone regularly offer guided float trips of the Madison. If you sign up for one of these trips you should plan to spend the entire day at it, because the boats are put in at an upper junction and you won't get out until near day's end somewhere downstream, a place at which a second car has been parked to get you back to your starting point.

Because the Madison is known for its stoneflies, especially the large

Pteronarcys californica, the fishing of stonefly nymph imitations is usually the rule. While it is possible to cast dry flies to certain lies as the boat
is drifted or maneuvered downstream, such casting is generally not the
best method of fishing the river, simply because there isn't enough time
to concentrate on such an area before the boat sweeps past it. A good guide
can, of course, try to hold the boat in place for you, but after a few such
occasions even he may suggest that you try a stonefly nymph, or at least
wait to use your dry flies until the boat can be stopped at one of the many
wadeable stretches that you'll come across on your way downstream.

Rods used on float trips are generally in the 9-foot class, and capable
of carrying a size 7 or 8 line. Sink-tip or full-sinking lines are the rule,
since you will be covering some of the deeper holes and pockets, and it is
an absolute must that your nymph pass along the bottom as the boat drifts
by. The nymphs used on such trips are also weighted.

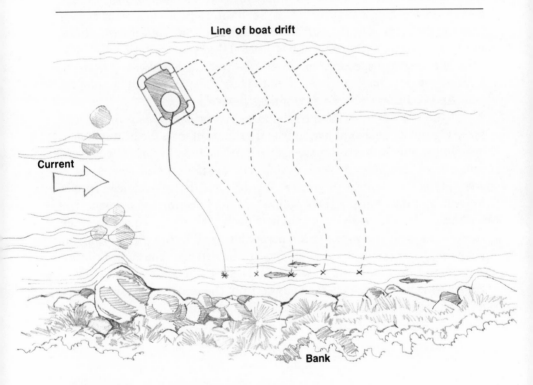

Figure 5–6. Casting while boat fishing.

Regardless of where you sit in your boat, a good guide will maneuver it so that you'll be in position to make the proper casts. He'll also suggest where you should place your fly, since he's been over the area many times and knows which spots have produced in the past.

The cast itself will be made downstream, or quartering downstream toward certain lies near shore, as shown in Figure 5–6. This will allow the fly line, leader, and fly to sink to the bottom while the boat is drifting or being maneuvered toward or past the area being fished. The current will also be pushing the leader, line, and fly along at a very natural pace. This float-drift method actually lets you drift your fly quite naturally past many fish for an almost indefinite period of time. For this type of fishing, a fairly short leader is recommended.

When float-drift fishing, you will need to control your fly line so that you always have just enough slack to keep your fly drifting naturally, but not so much that when you make the strike you have to take up more than the rod can handle properly. In other words you should be just a shade away from working a taut line. A pause, hesitation, or movement of your line going contrary to the current will indicate that you're either hung up on the bottom, or that a trout has decided that your imitation is at least worthy of closer inspection. In either case you must strike. If you've got a trout, you only have to play him to the boat. The guide will net him for you. And in big waters, all good guides have a net.

If you happen to be fishing such large rivers as the Madison on your own, without a guide or at least a friend to help out with the boat maneuvers, things will be a little more difficult. In such cases you will have to concentrate not only on your fishing, but on the type of water you're crossing as well. Nor will you be able to pick the best of lies, simply because you may not see them before you're almost on top of them. For the most part, the best you'll be able to do is take your chances with the current and fish the water that's accessible to you. You'll take fish, but not as well as if someone were sharing a boat with you. You can, of course, stop more often and fish those likely looking places by wading them. Either way, just being able to get away from the readily accessible places and fish where the average angler can't is exciting.

POINTS TO REMEMBER

- A long rod (9 feet) is preferable because you have more control over the line.
- Concentrate on the line, its movements and its pauses. Any deviation from the natural flow may be a fish. Strike.
- Use a line and leader that will let you get your fly to the bottom. Weight the fly if necessary.
- Learn to cover all the water on a given stretch of stream.
- In "big waters" use a HiD sink-tip line or a shooting head line to get to the bottom. "Walk" your nymph downstream and add line, to obtain a drag-free float, if necessary.
- In small streams cast directly upstream and let the nymph bounce along the bottom, on its way back to you, while you retrieve slack excess line.
- Try floating inaccessible waters in order to cover some of the best lies. Have either a friend or guide with you for the best maneuverability.

6

THE SECRET OF
THE WHITE NYMPH

THE SECRET OF THE WHITE NYMPH! That sounds like the title of a novel by Rider Haggard or a juvenile about the Hardy Boys. But we're dealing with fact, not fiction, and the fact is that a nymph periodically turns white as it grows, a significant phenomenon of nature that has thus far escaped the attention of many fly fishermen and fly tyers everywhere.

To grow, the nymphs or larvae of any insect species must shed their outer skins by molting. After they molt, they become colorless. We first discovered this some years ago when we were flipping over rocks in search of stonefly nymphs in Bailey's Brook, a tributary of the New Croton Reservoir in southern New York. Much to our astonishment, we picked up a nymph of *Acroneuria* that was white, a creamy white. We wondered if it were some kind of albino. Several days later, we found a similar nymph in the same brook, so we phoned our entomological mentor, Dr. Dominick J. Pirone. "Whenever insects shed their outer skin by molting," Dom explained, "they are pale or colorless for perhaps several hours. Their bodies are also very soft until the new outer skin hardens. Look into the entomological literature, and you'll find references to this." We looked. In *Insects, the Yearbook of Agriculture, 1952,* Frank H. Babers and John J. Pratt, Jr., wrote that "when first laid down, the new cuticle is soft and often colorless, but it rapidly hardens and assumes its normal color." In the revised sixth edition of *The Principles of Insect Physiology,* published in 1965, Sir Vincent Wigglesworth (what a great name to cite as an authority on nymphs) wrote, "The cuticle of the newly moulted insect is generally colourless, always quite soft. During the next hour or so it hardens and darkens."

But the angling literature, voluminous as it is, was another story. We searched book after book, author by author, and came up empty except for a brief mention of the white phase by J. R. Harris in *An Angler's Entomology,* originally published in London in 1952. "The colour of the newly-moulted nymph is at first a pale translucent whitish but it gradually darkens," Harris wrote. "The new exposed epicuticle remains soft for a short time. . . ." Even so, Harris did not recommend or suggest that an imitation white nymph should be tied or fished.

We decided to tie up some of our own. A soft, white nymph might be just the ticket for trout. We had reason to believe this might just be the case. After all, smallmouth bass dearly love a soft crayfish, and striped bass glut themselves on shedder crabs. We tied some white stonefly nymphs, size 10, using cream-colored latex for the body and wing cases, and white rubber for the antennae and tails. We had just gotten the latex from Raleigh Boaze, Jr., in Brunswick, Maryland, and although Ral had yet to publish on the subject, he and his friend Don Cooper were having a ball with trout using cream latex caddis imitations. Privately we wondered if the trout weren't gobbling up the caddis imitations under the impression that they were the molting nymphs of mayflies or stoneflies. The overwhelming majority of caddis larvae that are off-white or cream colored, are case makers, and trout rarely get to see them without their "houses" on.

Off we went to a nearby stream, the lower Croton River, a tributary of the Hudson. There are no stoneflies in the lower Croton because of irregular release of water from the dam impounding the New Croton Reservoir up above, but the cream-white stonefly nymphs worked on brown trout. For the hell of it, we tied an improbable emergent caddis pupa, size 10, in cream latex, and cast it, in full view of the fish, in the tiny pool at the very foot of the dam on a humid August afternoon. Bam, a 10-inch brown whacked it just 15 feet from us. The trout must have felt the point of the hook, but bam, it whacked the fly again. We were so thrilled by the brown's spunkiness that we took the fish home, dumped

Figure 6–1. *Acroneuria* nymphs before and after molting.

it into a 120-gallon aquarium (where it bullied largemouth bass), fed it
lavishly for a year, and then put it back into the pool whence it came. We
also fished the lower portion of the Croton, where the river is tidal, with
white stonefly nymphs and caught all the white perch and small striped
bass anyone would want.

Perhaps the fish took the nymphs because they had encountered
white nymphs of other insects. Or perhaps they took them because the
nymphs were conspicuous in the water and soft in the mouth. A white
nymph really stands out, and we began to ponder why we had devoted so
many hours to tying slavish imitations of the ordinary nymph that evolution has camouflaged for its protection. Maybe by tying realistic
Acroneuria, a dab of yellow in the second wing case here, a touch of brown
—ahhh, not too much—in the pronotum, and so on, we were doing ourselves in by concealing the nymph. Whatever was transpiring, the fish
took the white nymphs.

We continued our research. We talked to aquatic entomologists, we
ransacked the literature, and we attempted to figure out just how aware
fish, especially trout, might be of the white nymphs. Did they nose them
out? Did they smell them? Did they see them?

The newly molted nymph, we learned, is very secretive. It has to be.
It is a succulent snack for a fish. It is also very conspicuous. It hides under
rocks or takes other deep shelter. It doesn't move. In fact it can't move.
A live, ordinary *Acroneuria* nymph will scamper across your hand or up
your arm. In the white, rubbery phase it just lies there helpless. But if
they don't move about, how would trout know about these nymphs?

Maybe they get washed out by heavy water. Who knows? We kept digging. Molting is supposed to occur at night. But white at night would be even more conspicuous than during daylight if the nymph hadn't gained full shelter. Besides, we had collected our original white nymphs during the glory of the morning sun.

We turned over more rocks. True, it's not easy to find a white *Acroneuria.* You have to be lucky and be at the right spot at the right time. Either that or lift up several tons of rocks. But that's because *Acroneuria* is a predator and thus not as numerous as those species that feed on detritus. In the streams we examined, we found cream or light tan (apparently the next color phase as the darkening process continues) *Peltoperla* nymphs by the score in leaf packs. But how often did a newly molted *Peltoperla* get dislodged from a leaf pack? As we noted in chapter 3, trout will actually nose around in leaf litter for the species. But who knows if they were looking for the white ones? In any event, the white ones would surely stand out.

We tossed all of these questions back and forth. It is very tempting to look for evidence to support your discovery, or your theory, or your hypothesis, but we kept testing ours, and have come to the belief that trout are aware of the white nymph as a part of their stream environment. We know that a considerable superstructure of fishing theory—yea, dogma—can be built on the foundation of hot air, but consider the statistical probabilities.

Let's take one species of stonefly that has been studied in detail. *Neoperla clymene,* widely distributed in North America, will fit the bill. George L. Vaught and Ken Stewart, who examined the life history of this species (as we reported in chapter 3), found the standing crop of nymphs in a riffle to be 225 per square meter in May, just prior to emergence. There were undoubtedly more nymphs than this earlier in the year, because predation thins the population. But let us be conservative and use the figure of 225 nymphs per square meter as a population constant. The nymphs of *N. clymene* take a year to mature, and during that year they go through 23 instars. Again let's be conservative and say that there are only 20 times when each nymph molts; 20 is a nice round figure. Take away the month that the species is in the egg stage, do a little arithmetic, and you'll find that the nymph molts almost twice a month before emerging as an adult.

But let's continue. Say each molt takes an hour, so that the nymph is white, or creamy white, for 2 hours out of every month. The nymphs don't all molt at the same time or on the same day. The molting is random;

it's scattered in time. That means that there will be about 450 hours in every month when members of the *N. clymene* nymph population are going to be white. But that's over only one square meter of bottom. For 100 square meters of bottom, the total is 45,000 hours of white nymph time in a month. A month has 720 hours, so divide 720 into 45,000, and the answer is that you can expect to find 62 white nymphs of *N. clymene* in 100 square meters of stream bottom at any one time. True, the 62 white nymphs will be hiding, but some might become dislodged. And that figure of 62 is just for one species of stonefly alone. We can expect other molting stonefly species to be present in the same stream, and the same applies to mayfly nymphs and other insects. To a trout nosing the bottom, a white nymph should be no stranger.

We asked Ken Stewart for his opinion, and he said, "The average fish probably has an almost constant encounter with molting insects of its prey species. It's likely that nymphs are molting every day in every month of the year. The question now is, how many does the fish see? Here we're getting into the realm of the unknown. In predator-prey interaction, you have constant adjustments." Tom Waters said that "the appropriate behavior for the molting nymphs is to get into places where they are less vulnerable. All things equal, the chances of a trout getting a newly molted nymph are less than they would be for the normal instar. There are probably situations where the newly molted nymph gets moved from a secreted spot and becomes fair game. It's more visible."

We told several anglers about the white nymph phase. Angus Cameron, our editor at Knopf, got excited. Our explanation of the white nymph answered a question that had puzzled him for a long time. It turned out that some years back, Angus had started fishing a white nymph, exactly why and under what circumstances he couldn't recall, but it had worked exceptionally well indeed. "I used to pick over raffia bundles to find the lightest color I could get," Angus said. "I even tried to lighten them with peroxide. I also fished brown, green, and black raffia nymphs, but when I had guests and wanted to bring home fish, I invariably stuck to the white nymph."

"One episode in the Adirondacks sticks out," Angus continued, "and I suppose it was because it was the first time a nephew-in-law had ever fished with a fly rod for trout. I took him to a fly-fishing-only stretch on the East Branch of the Ausable. Self-conscious as a novice, my nephew insisted that I fish first, and I put on a white raffia nymph and took two rainbows right off. Meantime, he had tied on a dark green nymph on a second rod of mine, waded in, and under tutelage was soon making per-

Figure 6–2. White Nymph.

fectly executed slightly upstream casts and then fishing them out down-stream. He didn't raise a fish. Thinking that the most likely reason was that he was not seeing the take, I waded out, took his rod, and fished through the stretch without raising a fish either. Leaving him in the river, I waded ashore, exchanged rods, and waded back to him with the rod on which I had taken the fish. This time I brought my fly box with me, for I had left my vest on shore. It was a good thing, because on the very first cast of the white nymph, my nephew, to his utter surprise, hooked a fish and promptly popped the tippet. He tied on another white nymph, and he caught three fish right off. From then on I didn't try to discover whether the fish would take other nymphs. The two of us stuck to white raffia and were still fishing and taking fish until it got dark."

Ted Niemeyer was similarly pleased when we told him about the white nymph. "That explains something," Ted said. "Some years ago while fishing the Green River in Wyoming, I fished a white quill nymph that I had just happened to tie while experimenting one day. It was an imitation of *Pteronarcys californica*. I cast it out, and one of the biggest fish I have ever had on took it. The fish broke off finally with the nymph, but now I can understand why the white nymph worked. I think the white nymph is a great idea."

Charlie Brooks was intrigued. He tied up a white nymph in the round, calling it the Alabaster Nymph, and began fishing it in late 1979. He used it in combination with his black Montana Stone, one on the end of the leader, the other on a dropper. He kept switching them around to assure impartiality. "I had the damndest season I ever had," Charlie said. "I must have lost 25 fish, nice fish, and I couldn't tell which nymph they had struck. Of the fish I did land, I landed half on the Alabaster Nymph, half on the Montana Stone." Charlie said that he was going to try the two nymphs in tandem again. "Maybe the Alabaster Nymph will work better earlier in the season," he said.

You don't have to wait for Charlie to report further on his experiments with the white nymph. You can tie up your own, using fur or latex to make it soft. You be the judge, and let us know what happens.

7

TYING AND FISHING THE ADULT STONEFLY

> The stonefly is to trout what filet
> mignon is to man.
>
> —Lenox Dick, *The Art and Science of Fly Fishing*

TYING A BIG DRY STONEFLY on a long-shanked hook calls for materials that will float well. Unfortunately, most of the big flies on the market won't perform in rough water unless they are constantly overloaded with fly dope, and even then they sink. Floatability is critical.

The fly we're going to show you now, K's Butt

Salmonfly, is a new fly that has been thoroughly tested in Montana waters by a number of anglers. It is lethal. Trout don't put on the brakes to inspect it. They slam into it. But one angler had a complaint. He said the two flies he used had sunk. Sunk? This fly should float forever. "Yeah, they sunk," he said. "I got four fish, 16 to 20 inches, and they punctured them." We take all criticism seriously, so we have since strengthened the body by giving it several applications of "Hard as Nails" fingernail polish, and we sometimes insert flat cork sheeting inside the quill to fill up the body. We expect K's Butt Salmonfly to become the standard dry version of the adult *Pteronarcys californica* in the West. Elsewhere in the country, it can be adapted to simulate other adult *Pteronarcys* or *Allonarcys* species.

When you fish this fly, be prepared for sudden strikes by big fish. We mean big fish that 3X leaders won't hold. Listen to these comments from Charlie Brooks: "Well, I must tell you," Charlie began. "A friend and I took those flies you sent and went down to Varney Bridge on the Madison. We had a roaring day. There weren't many flies out, which I've always said is the best, since the trout can't be so choosy. The trout were feeding at the edge of *very* fast water, they'd chase the damn fly downstream, hit it going like an express train and just keep on going when they felt the hook. Some were too big to force back upstream even with 12-pound test leaders. We hooked maybe 40, landed about 15, all 18 inches or smaller. We just couldn't handle the big fish (four to five pounders) in that fast water. The fast tearing runs just shook my old 1495 Medalist reel apart. Screws all came loose, lost one. Damndest day I ever had with running trout. They savaged those flies. Bit the ends of bodies off, chewed off wings, legs. But as long as they floated the fish kept hitting them, even with just the quill body left."

Although the tying procedure may at first appear complicated, it really is not. In fact, K's Butt Salmonfly is much easier to tie than the Sofa Pillow, Bird's Stonefly, or other patterns that anglers have fished over the years. Moreover, in the words of one of our field testers, Max Warr, it will outfish the other patterns by 10 to 1. Try it. Remember, you read it here first.

K's BUTT SALMONFLY (Figure 7–1)

HOOK SIZE: 2 to 6 (Mustad #36620)
THREAD: Flymaster 6/0 orange, pre-waxed
BODY: Butt end of a peacock quill stem for abdomen, same for
    thorax, which has a layer of thin cork sheeting over it
SEGMENTATION: Black size D tying thread
HEAD: Forward end of peacock quill stem
TAILS: Two strands of dark rubber hackle
LEGS: Six strands of dark rubber hackle knotted
WINGS: Two mallard flank feathers dipped in Pliobond
ANTENNAE: Two strands of dark rubber hackle

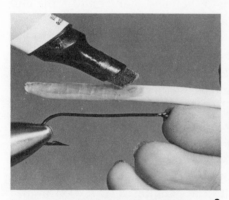
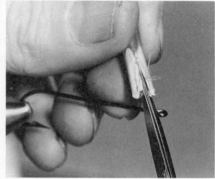

a

b

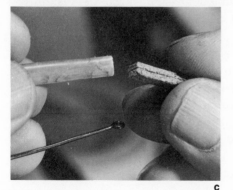

c

Figure 7–1. Tying the K's Butt Salmonfly. (*a*) Coloring the peacock quill
orange. (*b*) Notching pith in peacock
quill. (*c*) Inserting cork strips in hollow quill.

Take the butt end of a stripped peacock quill shaft and color it orange with a #150M Pantone marking pen (a). Apply fingernail polish over the coloring and let dry. When we tie K's Butt, we usually color and apply polish on a dozen of the flies at a time, so that the bodies we tie are dry and the ink won't run off when the flies are handled. If the orange isn't deep enough for you, you can always color the body again with the Pantone pen, even after the fly is completed, because the black thread used for segmentation won't take up the orange ink.

Next, notch the pith in the forward end of the butt so that it can slip over the forward end of the hook shank (b). If the butt has no pith, insert one or two strips of flat cork inside the quill (c). We sometimes do this, as we noted above, to make the body more durable, even if the quill has pith.

Spiral tying thread onto the hook shank behind the eye and coat it with nail polish (d).

Place the slit in the quill butt onto the hook shank and tie the butt to the shank, winding thread over the first third of the body (e). This area will form the thorax and head. Color again with a Pantone marker if you wish. The tying thread will take up the ink.

Cut a piece of cork sheeting approximately three-eighths of an inch wide so that it extends forward from the end of the thorax to just short of the head, as shown (f). Be sure to leave a one-eighth inch space for the head. Now tie down the cork on top of the quill, color the cork with the Pantone marker, and apply nail polish (g,h).

Next, tie in a section of size D black thread behind the cork thorax and then bring this thread rearward straight over the back to the tail, securing it on top of the abdomen with the tying thread (i,j). Don't worry about the orange tying thread showing up over the black; the instant you touch it up with the Pantone pen it will blend in. Tie off and remove the hook from the vise.

Now insert the hook in the vise so that it is held by the eye. This is an optional step, but we like tails on our stoneflies, even though they're not necessary. Tie in the tails of dark rubber hackle as shown (k).

Take the tying thread forward to the thorax, and now spiral the black segmenting thread forward toward the thorax 9 or 10 times (l,m).

Clip off any excess black thread, apply nail polish so that the thread won't slip, and let dry (n). If you wish, use the Pantone orange marker yet again. The black thread won't take up the color. The abdomen is now complete.

Prepare six rubber legs of dark rubber hackle by knotting individual

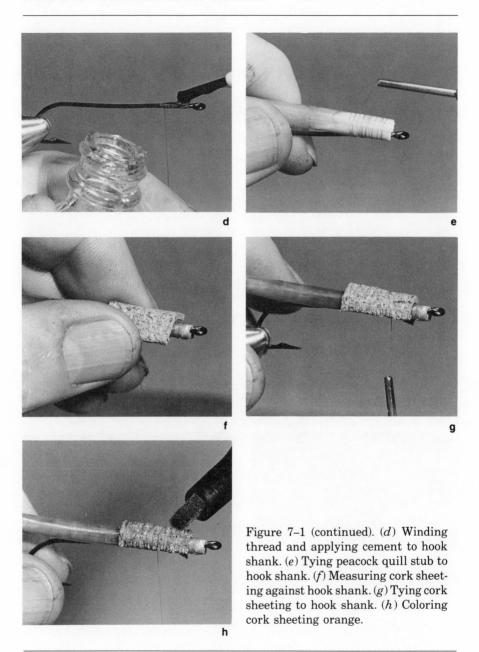

Figure 7–1 (continued). (*d*) Winding thread and applying cement to hook shank. (*e*) Tying peacock quill stub to hook shank. (*f*) Measuring cork sheeting against hook shank. (*g*) Tying cork sheeting to hook shank. (*h*) Coloring cork sheeting orange.

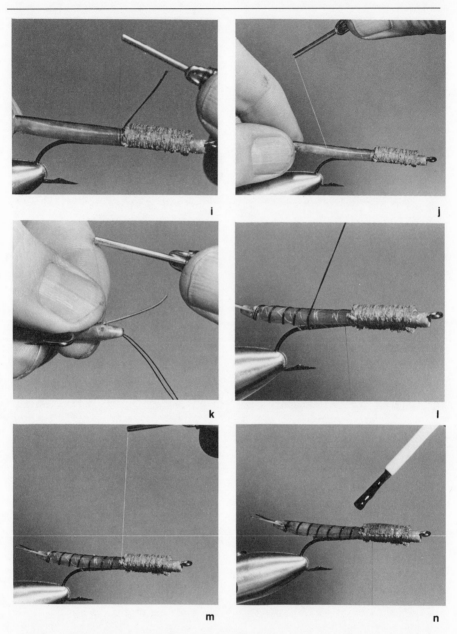

Figure 7–1 (continued). (*i*) Tying in size D black thread. (*j*) Securing size D black thread along top of quill. (*k*) Tying in rubber hackle tail. (*l*) Winding size D black thread forward to form segmentation. (*m*) The segmented body formed. (*n*) Applying polish to peacock quill and thread windings.

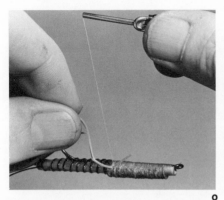
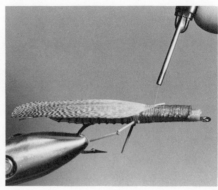

o

p

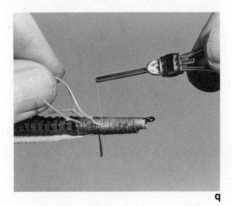

q

Figure 7-1 (continued). (*o*) Tying in first set of rubber legs. (*p*) Tying in first mallard wing. (*q*) Tying in second set of legs.

strands. When we first tied this fly, we simply wound dark brown or black hackle over the area to serve as legs; but even though this fly caught trout to beat the band, we wanted to be more realistic.

Tie in the first pair of legs beneath the thorax just where the cork topping ends (*o*). The legs should extend outward. Snip off excess rubber butts, then cement the tying thread with nail polish.

Take two mallard flank feathers and dip them in Pliobond. They will dry quickly. Both feathers, one slightly longer than the other, should extend beyond the tails.

Next, place the shorter of the two mallard feathers on top of the thorax just ahead of the legs, tie it securely into place, and apply nail polish (*p*).

Tie in the second pair of legs one at a time, three-sixteenths of

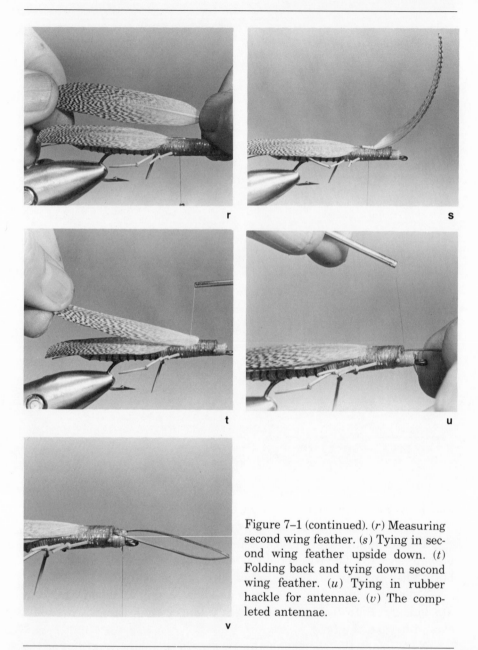

Figure 7–1 (continued). (r) Measuring second wing feather. (s) Tying in second wing feather upside down. (t) Folding back and tying down second wing feather. (u) Tying in rubber hackle for antennae. (v) The completed antennae.

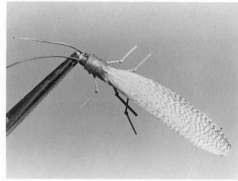

w

x

y

Figure 7–1 (continued). (*w, x, y*) Three
views of the completed fly.

an inch forward of the first pair, snip the butt ends, and apply nail polish (*q*).

Now tie in the second wing feather upside down, as shown. When you bend it backwards, it should match the other wing feather in length (*r,s,t*). We first tie this feather in upside down because when it is pulled back, the forward portion that lies flat looks exactly like the full wing of the living fly. This is absolutely unnecessary to deceive a trout, but then we like to deceive ourselves, and we can fish the fly with just that much more faith in it. Carrying our insanity further, in a step that we don't show here, we tie this feather down with transparent thread so that no color shows on top where the feather is folded backwards. And the same to you, Jack!

Tie in the third and last set of legs equidistant from the other two pairs. This pair should lie just where the pronotum begins. If you want to get a more mathematical measure into your mind, imagine that the thorax is divided into thirds, which, in the living fly, it is.

Tie in the antennae of dark rubber. If you wish, dab on black lacquer for the eyes afterwards (u,v). You now have the completed fly.

You can simplify these steps, if you wish, merely by lashing an orange quill butt onto the hook shank, segmenting it with black thread, tying on just one wing that extends beyond the abdomen, and winding regular hackle around the thorax. On the other hand, we sometimes may make the pattern more involved and more realistic by adding a pronotum and marking it fore and aft with bright size D orange thread to resemble the fleshy parts found in the living adult. There are certain other steps we take to make the pattern almost indiscernible from the real life *Pteronarcys,* but if we told you what they were, you'd clamor to have us locked up. We also tie the K's Butt Salmonfly nymph (see Plate 1).

YOU CAN USE quill butts from smaller feathers to tie up just about any adult stonefly. Recently we used a quill butt from a duck primary to make a very realistic K's Butt *Acroneuria* complete with mono eyes and bent legs of goose biots touched with Pliobond to hold their shape (see Plate 2). We gave the fly to William Humphrey, author of *The Spawning Run* and *My Moby Dick*, and his wife, Dorothy. Several weeks later, Bill called and said excitedly, "Dorothy and I were guests of Ted Thomas and his wife, Sally, on a private club stream in Pennsylvania. My beat was a half mile of water, and I went through it without doing anything on standard dry flies. Then I started fishing downstream using the K's Butt. On four casts I caught four fish about fourteen inches, three rainbows and one brown. The next day my friend Ted Thomas used it, and he caught twenty-four fish from twelve to sixteen inches, browns, brooks and rainbows. He gave the fly to Sally, and she tossed it in the torrent below the club dam. A fish twenty-eight to thirty inches long came out of nowhere and seized it. She didn't land it because she didn't keep constant pressure on, but she and Ted saw it. Hey, send me a dozen of those flies."

GARY BORGER AND ourselves have independently come up with almost identical ties of ultra-durable and high-floating *Pteronarcys*. The pattern is very easy to tie, and the material colors can be changed to imitate other adult stoneflies. Here it is.

SALMONFLY (Figure 7–2)

HOOK SIZE: 4 to 6 (Mustad #79580)
THREAD: Dark brown Monocord
BODY: Clipped orange deer hair
RIBBING: Formed by palmered brown hackle and trimmed flush
THORAX: Clipped orange deer hair
WING: Woodchuck guard hairs
HACKLE: Dark brown hackle fibers

Place a size 4 hook in the vise and wrap the dark brown Monocord thread onto the shank near the bend. Monocord is strong and lies flat, and you can apply proper tension when spinning the deer hair. Most of the shank is left bare because this makes it easier to spin the deer hair.

Prepare a long brown hackle feather as if you were going to tie a dry-fly hackle with it. Tie the trimmed butt end to the shank at the bend of the hook. The feather will later form the ribbing.

Snip a bunch of orange deer body hair about the diameter of a soda straw from the hide. Hold it parallel to the shank just above the bend and take two turns of thread around it (*a*). Tighten the thread. The tension causes the deer hair to flare. If the hair does not flare around all the thread wraps—and deer hair does not readily spin around the shank when tied over thread or other materials—take another bunch of hair, hold it over the bald patch, and tie it in with a couple of turns of thread. It will flare and cover the bald patch. Once you're past any bald patch, you're home free as far as flaring deer hair is concerned because the hair spins readily on a naked shank.

Continue tying on the deer hair until you get two-thirds of the way toward the eye of the hook, where the thorax is to start (*b*) When you reach this point, half-hitch the tying thread, remove the unfinished fly—a hairy orange ball—from the vise, and trim the deer hair to shape. Be sure not to cut off the saddle feather. When trimming the deer hair, try to make the abdomen flat on top and bottom and slightly rounded on the sides. This lets the fly float properly.

Near the thorax, trim the abdomen ultra-flat on top so that when the wing is tied in it will lie against the body and not flare upward at an angle.

After you finish trimming, reinsert the fly in the vise and wind the thread on the shank just in front of the abdomen.

Wind the hackle feather in an open spiral up to the thread and tie it down (*c*). Cut away the excess tip.

Use scissors to trim all of the hackle fibers flush with the abdomen. All that should remain is a visible brown line, forming segmentation markings from the rear to the front of the fly (*d*).

Now it's time to tie in the woodchuck fiber wing. Take the fibers from the back of a woodchuck. The guard hairs have a progressive barring of black, tan, and black with a white tip. Cut a section of these from the hide. Remove some of the underfur, *but not all of it.* By preventing the guard hairs from matting, the underfur enhances the impression of life when the fly is fished.

a   b

c   d

Figure 7–2. Tying the Salmonfly. (*a*) Deer hair flared on hook shank. (*b*) Deer hair spun on hook shank. (*c*) Winding hackle through clipped deer hair body. (*d*) The completed abdomen.

e   f

Figure 7–2 (continued). (*e*) Tying in woodchuck fiber as wing. (*f*) Tying in the two brown hackles.

Lay the guard hairs and underfur on top of the clipped deer hair body just rearward of its completion point. Tie the hairs in slightly off center to the far side.

Cut another section of guard hairs and tie this in also, but slightly off center to the near side. The effect you want is that of a full wing. There should be a slight tapering angle outward as the tips pass the bend of the hook. The tips of the guard hairs should extend past the bend for almost half an inch (*e*).

Do not trim the butts of the hairs too close to the tie-in point; leave about an eighth of an inch to be tied securely with thread. Woodchuck fibers are slippery and tend to pull out.

Tie in two dark brown saddle or neck hackle feathers at the completion point of the abdomen (*f*).

Take some more orange deer hair and spin it around the shank to form the thorax area (*g*). After you reach the eye of the hook, whip-finish your thread and remove the fly from the vise. Now trim the thorax area so as to make it appear a natural continuation of the abdomen (*h*). It should immediately begin to taper, being just a bit wider on the sides, before it narrows again for the head. When the trimming has been completed, reinsert the fly in your vise and reattach the thread.

Wind the saddle hackle feathers, one at a time, through the clipped thorax to the thread (*i*). The windings should be in a slightly open spiral.

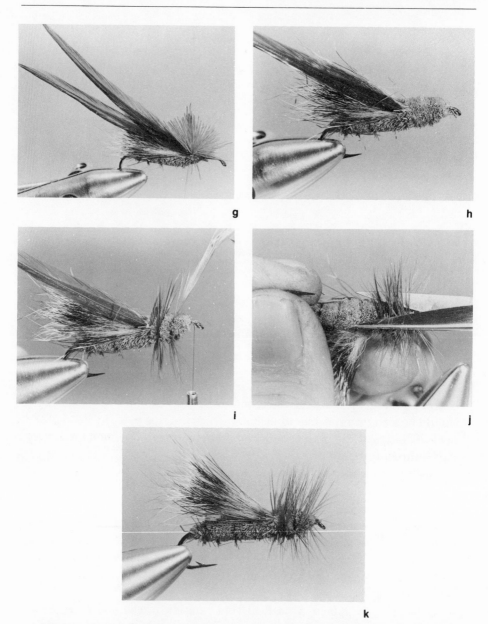

Figure 7–2 (continued). (*g*) Spinning more deer hair on hook for thorax. (*h*) The formed deer hair thorax. (*i*) Winding hackle through clipped deer hair thorax. (*j*) Trimming hackle on bottom of thorax. (*k*) The completed Salmonfly.

When the feathers have been wound through in dry-fly fashion, trim the excess, whip-finish, and touch off the windings with head lacquer (*j*).

Remove the fly from the vise and use scissors to trim the bottom hackle so that you form a V-shaped opening under the thorax. This will allow the fly to ride flush, with the correct silhouette, when fished.

We have fished this particular pattern in slow and fast water; it floats extremely well. The one thing you will notice is that the wing of woodchuck guard hairs seems to remain flush with the water surface and vibrates like a thing alive. When the fly is removed from the water the wing sleeks down into a solid wet mass. Yet when the fly again lands, on a new cast, out go the wings, throbbing in an enticing fashion.

THE ADULT IMITATION of *Pteronarcys californica* tied by Charles E. Brooks is very effective. Here is the description of the pattern.

BROOKS' SALMONFLY

HOOK SIZE: 4 to 6   (Mustad #79580)
THREAD: Black
ABDOMEN: Elk hair (or deer hair)
RIBBING: Dark brown saddle hackle feather trimmed to stubs, counterwound with waxed burnt orange floss. Segments run through thorax to head
WING: Wood duck flank feather
HACKLE: Dark brown hackle feathers

Charlie ties in the elk or deer hair lengthwise, surrounding the hook shank. The ribbing of hackle forming the segmentation is counterwound with waxed burnt orange floss. The single wing of the wood duck flank feather is simply laid over the back of the body.

FISHING THE DRY STONEFLY

Without question, the greatest stonefly hatches occur in the Rocky Mountains and the Pacific Northwest. The greatest hatch of all is that of *Pteronarcys californica*. It can be unbelievable. Emergence takes place mainly in May and June, although there are hatches on some rivers in July as well. Call ahead because timing is critical. What you want to catch is the head of the hatch, where salmonflies have begun to emerge in some numbers. Because the hatch moves upstream as the water warms, finding the head is a game. Weather conditions can speed up or slow down the hatch. To stay ahead in the game, Charlie Brooks turns over basketball-sized boulders in a foot of water at the edge of a river. "If I find a dozen nymphs under a boulder that size—and I have found as many as 30 or 40 —I'll know the nymphs will start to emerge in a day or so," Charlie says. "I'll go back to the location the next morning, and if the hatch hasn't started, I'll fish the nymph. When the fish start rising, I'll fish the dry."

If you fish the salmonfly hatch, forget about light tackle. You'll need at least an 8-foot rod and a size 7 or 8 floating line. The West is the land "where the wind blows free," the water is high in the big rivers, and wading is an adventure. On a gusty day, the salmonflies, clumsy fliers at best, might be all over the place, and so are the fish feeding on them. On other days, the fish might be inshore, right off the banks, gorging on the flies that drop from the willows. But no matter where the fish are, be prepared. Have a big rod and a gutsy reel with plenty of backing. There are big fish out there. These trout are not shy, and your leader need not be more than 3 feet. "They are not line shy either," says Charlie Brooks. "I've had them take with a leader only 10 inches long."

Eastern and Midwestern anglers who do not have the opportunity to fish the West should not despair. Study the streams you fish, and you may be surprised. For example, certain rivers in the upper Midwest, which our sources insist remain nameless, do have heavy flights of *Pteronarcys dorsata*. Another example: A big salmonfly imitation can be very effective on landlocked salmon in the West Branch of the Penobscot River in Maine in late June and early July. "It's nothing like a hatch out in Montana," says Ed Reif of Eddie's Flies in Bangor. "There's not a great big number of them, but you'll see those big *Pteronarcys* flying around. You can get some nice 3- to 4-pound fish on the big stonefly imitation, especially during a caddis hatch. I think the fish are looking for them, because they'll take them over the caddis."

Don't neglect the small stoneflies, particularly early in the season. The adults do not stand out because they are small and dark, but there may be more around than you think. One of the best places to check for them is on bridges. From late April to early May, Maine fishermen often use little black or little olive dry flies tied on a size 18, 2X long hook, and they do well, especially in the blueberry barrens of Washington County. "There are little ponds and irrigation ditches," says Ed Reif, "and they all have brook trout in them. You'll see the little stoneflies on bushes or

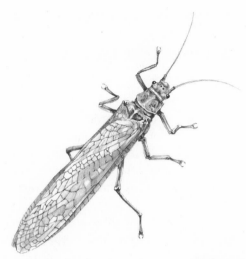

Figure 7–3. *Pteronarcys californica* adult.

flying around, and when they land on the water the fish will nail them. The little stonefly patterns work better than anything else."

Nationwide, much work remains to be done on stonefly emergence dates, but in the Appendix we present the latest emergence tables for various localities from coast to coast. Use them to your advantage.

Presentation

We like to use a rod of at least 8 feet, and preferably 9 feet when we do our dry-fly fishing with stonefly imitations. Length of rod and line weight are, of course, determined by the size of the stream. By using the longest rod possible on a given stream we have the advantage of line control, which is especially important in imparting motion to the fly when the dead-drift method doesn't produce. A long rod also makes the mending of a line much easier.

When fishing the Madison in Montana, or a similar river, during the salmonfly hatch and at the height of the emergence, almost anything goes. And, as we explained a few pages ago, you almost can't do anything wrong. Standard practice, however, requires a size 7 or 8 line on a 9-foot rod, and a 7½-foot leader tipping out at no less than 3X (approximately 5-pound test). Many anglers prefer to use a 2X and even a 1X tippet simply because the fly that is cast is large and turns over better with a gutsier tippet, besides which the heavier tippet can handle trophy-sized trout, which are not uncommon under the circumstances.

During those periods when the emergence is only sparse or mediocre, and the dead-drift float doesn't produce, we like we switch to the twitching method, which is the same method one would use during a caddis fly hatch. After the fly is cast on the water and allowed to drift for a few feet, the rod tip is lifted and twitched. The motion, if done properly, causes the fly to skitter on the surface of the stream for a few inches, giving the impression of an adult stonefly trying to take off. This action is also similar to that used by a bass fisherman after a bug has been cast and suddenly comes alive after a resting period, hopping across the surface for a short distance.

After the twitching motion has been made, the fly is allowed to drift downstream again, and as soon as drag sets in the method is repeated. We can't recall how many times this maneuver has produced vicious strikes when the conventional cast, float, and drift method has failed.

As described in the section on nymph fishing in big waters, in chapter 5, one of the casts we use quite often on rivers like the Madison is the upstream hold cast, which employs 6 or 7 feet of slack line off the reel. The rod tip is moved horizontally in an upstream direction when the cast is delivered to the target area, thus allowing a number of additional feet of drag-free float. Rivers like the Madison are known for their whimsical and varying current flows, and you must adjust and maneuver constantly to obtain an optimum presentation.

The salmonfly hatch of the West has the great advantage to the angler of occurring during daylight hours. This lets you see the rising fish and the fly. It is another matter entirely to fish the same type of pattern during darkness.

Night Fishing

Since most stoneflies are active at night, mating and laying eggs, this is also an excellent time to fish the adult imitations. In order to accomplish this properly you should first familiarize yourself thoroughly with the stream you're fishing, not only for the likeliest places where stoneflies are going to be fluttering about, but also for wading safety. Even familiar stream surroundings have an entirely different appearance after dark. At night the river becomes a mysterious and challenging hunting ground for both angler and trout. And in trout it brings out the bigger predators, the fish you didn't see or even suspect existed in the same water during the day.

The experienced night fisherman, like the Michigan anglers who go trout hunting during the hatch of *Hexagenia limbata* in late June, don't waste time or effort during the pre-hatch sunset hours. Most of them will pick their stations and only enter the water as the light begins to fail—unless, of course, too many anglers in the area force them into the stream earlier, in which case even they will protect their immediate territory. It's a first-come, first-placed situation.

We ran into one such stalwart on Michigan's South Branch of the Au Sable River, above Grayling. It was not quite dark but he was already in position in midstream, with a rod under his arm. He just stood there calmly, smoking an outsized cigar that made enough smoke to eliminate completely any need for insect repellent. We were walking down from an upstream position, searching for a likely place ourselves. What prompted us to stop and talk to this stalwart was that a number of fish were rising in various areas well within casting distance of the station he'd chosen. We asked him why he didn't fish to the obviously rising trout.

"Hey," he replied, "if you want to fish to those brookies be my guest. I'm not about to get my line wet on them. The 'Hex' should be off in about half an hour. You boys better get set before the real action starts."

This angler knew exactly what he was doing. He knew where the fish would be working during the emergence. And though he wouldn't be able to see the flies or the rising trout, he knew exactly how much line he would need to reach them. It was also a matter of remaining silent so that each slurp and splash could be detected. Those anglers experienced in night fishing took fish. Those unfamiliar with it didn't, except for the occasional lucky cast made at the right time and place.

When night fishing for trout, whether with an adult stonefly imitation or whatever else, you should first find a proper station and be in position at least 20 minutes before you actually begin to fish. It is preferable to have fished the area during daylight, so that you know just how much distance you'll have to cast. A little trick we like to use is to wrap two turns of fine thread around the fly line to indicate how many feet of line are through the guides. We don't like to use any kind of light during the fishing itself, since this puts down the fish (but you don't have any choice if you have to change flies). By practicing a few casts during daylight, you also learn how much time passes before your line begins to drag and before you'll have to make a new presentation.

As you stand in your position in the dark you'll hear the sounds of fish working. Generally, the stations picked for night fishing are in such areas of the stream that the sounds can be heard. You won't hear very much if your station is at the head of fast-moving riffle water above a pool. This may be a fine area in which trout will lie during daylight, but things change at night. Then, trout, especially larger ones, move out of secluded lies and go on the prowl through the slower and shallower waters in search of prey.

Even if your ears don't detect a rising fish, you should make an occasional cast with your fly. The stonefly imitation you'll be using will not only look like the insect you've tried to represent, but like other forms of insect life as well. During the dark hours there are moths and caddis that also fly around; when these fall into the water, a trout doesn't really care what they are—food is food. And what difference does it make to an angler what the trout take his imitation for as long as they take it.

When you fish during the evening and predawn hours, you'll also want to use a leader that's heavier than the one you would normally use. Because you won't be able to see where a hooked fish is going, you can't let him roam at will, since he may take you under logs or various snags. You have to be in full control of the fish, and that requires the much stronger connection that a heavier leader gives you. The Michigan anglers who fish the *Hexagenia* hatch simply tie on 10-pound-test tippets and almost horse the fish to the net. (The South Branch of the Au Sable in that state is strewn with submerged logs, and if you let a fish run, you lose him.)

After you have made a cast in the darkness it will be only by guessing, and hopefully educated guessing, that you'll know where your fly is. If you can detect an audible rise in the form of a splash or slurp in the vicinity of your fly, you'll have to strike. The strike, itself, however, should not be overly sharp. If you strike so hard that you pull your line from the water, who knows where you may tangle it or the leader. No, the strike should be firm yet controlled. Once you feel the fish, a second strike with the rod tip will assure penetration of the hook point.

The twitching method à la caddis or stonefly is also very effective during darkness, since it will give the impression of a fallen insect trying to escape the force of the current.

Small Streams

The adult stonefly imitation is also an excellent choice for small streams (20 feet wide or less) since many such streams are overhung with tree branches and bushes, and are generally alive with insect life. Since stoneflies look much like grasshoppers, caddis flies, and other insects when silhouetted from below the stream surface, they make for an all-purpose imitation that can be fished whether fish are rising or not. And, as we mentioned earlier, the size of the stream doesn't determine the size of the natural stonefly. Some streams no more than 4 feet wide will harbor 2-inch specimens of *Allonarcys biloba*.

We fish the small variety of stream with a short rod because of the overhang usually present. The rod in this case should be stiff enough to cast the large imitations; a size 5 line with a 3X tippet on a 7½-foot leader seems to handle well. Rods of 6½ or 7 feet are sometimes the longest that can be handled without constantly hanging up the tip in bushes or tree limbs.

Fishing is most easily accomplished by means of the upstream or quartering upstream cast. This allows for a quiet approach as the various pockets and holding lies are covered. The twitching maneuver is not easily accomplished on an upstream cast, since the current is constantly pushing the fly back at you. You will have to retrieve excess line continuously in order to keep a fairly straight line between you and the fly, so that when you strike you don't have to take up too much slack.

SUMMARY OF POINTS TO REMEMBER

- When tying adult stonefly imitations, use materials that float yet give the lifelike impression of the natural.
- Use as long a rod as the stream will permit for full control of the fly and leader.
- In addition to fishing your fly dead-drift, try twitching the fly as though it were trying to get off the surface.
- When fishing at night, first familiarize yourself with the area so you know the water by memory, and how much line you'll need. Use a leader heavier than the one you would use in daylight.

8

STONEFLY PATTERNS, NYMPHS AND ADULTS FOR ALL SEASONS, COAST TO COAST

GIANT BLACK NATURE NYMPH (Plate 1)
Craig Mathews, West Yellowstone, Montana

PTERONARCYS CALIFORNICA

WINTER, SPRING, SUMMER, AND FALL

HOOK SIZE: 2 to 8 (Mustad #9575, barb mashed down)
THREAD: Black 3/0 Monocord
TAILS: Goose or turkey pointer quills dyed orange
WEIGHTED FOUNDATION: Strips of #4 fuse wire laid along sides of hook shank. Additional weight may be added by wrapping #2 fuse wire over foundation

ABDOMEN TOP AND SIDES: Dark brown seal or imitation seal

ABDOMEN BELLY: Strip of orange-dyed angora

RIBBING: #21 Swannundaze, dark brown, or deep brown 20-pound-test flat monofilament

WING PADS: Chocolate-brown-dyed heavy latex cut to shape, front case cut longer for pronotum and head

THORAX: Same as abdomen top and sides

LEGS: Amber-dyed church-window pheasant feathers

PRONOTUM: Front wing case pulled over top of thorax

HEAD: Black Monocord over latex from pronotum

ANTENNAE: Same as tails

Craig Mathews, the chief of police in West Yellowstone, also guides and ties flies for Bud Lilly. He says, "I fish all my stonefly nymphs upstream dead drift, and I fish them 12 months a year. Stomach pump surveys show *Pteronarcys californica* nymphs present in the fish all year long. When the nymphs are emerging, I fish the nymph right next to shore where the fish are waiting. In fairly still waters, the nymph rides upside down, but in heavy currents the nymph tumbles, and this is the desired effect. In midwinter, we wait 'til 12 noon to fish the nymph, with noon to 4 in the afternoon being the most effective time."

CLAASSENIA NYMPH (Plate 3)
David Quammen, Ennis, Montana

CLAASSENIA SABULOSA

WINTER, SPRING, SUMMER, AND FALL

HOOK SIZE: 4 (Mustad #79580)

TYING THREAD: Grayish tan Monocord, waxed

WEIGHT: .035-inch lead wire

TAILS: .010-inch round monofilament dyed brown

RIBBING: 20-pound-test flat monofilament (Cortland Cobra) dyed brown

ABDOMEN: Olive-gold acrylic crewel yarn

THORAX: Large, grayish tan chenille

LEGS: Mallard flank dyed to "wood duck"

HEAD: Tying thread

A writer and guide, Quammen says that "this is one of my two year-round bread-and-butter nymphs. The other is a size 12 light brown caddis pupa. If I had to spend a full year in the Montana woods feeding myself on trout or starving and could take just two patterns, I'd take the *Claassenia* nymph and the caddis pupa. The *Claassenia* works very well on the Madison and especially in the Madison Channels, my home ballpark, summer or winter. The Channels, a wonderland of variety water with Madison richness, does *not,* for some reason have much *Pteronarcys californica.* Instead there are mucho *Claassenia,* and hence the value of this nymph."

LITTLE BLACK STONEFLY NYMPH (Plate 4)
Jay Neve, Bellevue, Michigan, and Don Fox, Chassel, Michigan

CAPNIIDAE NYMPH

WINTER AND EARLY SPRING

HOOK SIZE: 10 to 18 (Mustad #9671 or #9672)
THREAD: Black
TAILS: Dark brown goose biots
BODY: Black mink or muskrat dubbing covering a neatly tapering body of lead tying thread
WING PADS: Goose quill segments (dyed or Pantone black)
LEGS: Black hen hackle
ANTENNAE: Dark brown goose biots

POLY-CADDIS STYLE FLY (Plate 4)
Gary Borger, Wausau, Wisconsin

CAPNIIDAE, TAENIOPTERYGIDAE, NEMOURIDAE, LEUCTRIDAE, PERLODIDAE, AND CHLOROPERLIDAE ADULTS

WINTER, SPRING, AND EARLY SUMMER

HOOK SIZES: 12 to 16 (Mustad #9672) and 10 to 16 (Mustad #94840)
THREAD: Pre-waxed Monocord, matching color
TAIL: None
BODY: Dubbed fur

HACKLE: Wind over thorax and trim top and bottom, color to match body

WING: Polypropylene yarn tied in at head; trim butt end of wing a little long to form a slight clump which is not wound under; place a drop of head cement on the clump; color of wing to match body

MOST USED COLORS: Black, dark brown, bright yellow, chartreuse

Borger says, "On those few streams that are open to trout fishing during the winter months, the black to rusty brown nymphs of the families Capniidae and Taeniopterygidae are significant. Adult colors are similar to those of the nymphs. Emergence occurs in the early autumn and the adults often pepper the snow banks like particles of soot. Trout will rise freely to adults that are on the water to lay eggs."

"Members of the families Nemouridae and Leuctridae are dull gray to brown in color," he explains. "Adults emerge and lay eggs after dark throughout the warm seasons. Adults of these two families can on occasion be abundant enough to bring the fish to the surface at dusk, especially on smaller, rocky streams populated by brook trout."

"The bright yellow to chartreuse members of the families Perlodidae and Chloroperlidae are widespread in swift, rocky streams," notes Borger. Adults emerge after dark, but egg laying is often a daytime activity. Trout seem well acquainted with these 'Yellow Sally' stoneflies and will rise eagerly to them."

TAENIOPTERYX NYMPH (Plate 4)
Dave McNeese, Salem, Oregon

WINTER AND SPRING

HOOK SIZE: 14 to 16 (Mustad #9671)
THREAD: Brown
TAILS: Dark brown feather sections
OVERBODY: Dark brown feather section
UNDERBODY: Dark brown fur dubbing
RIBBING: Brown thread
WING CASE: Dark brown feather section
LEGS: Dark brown feather fibers

TAENIOPTERYX ADULT
Dave McNeese, Salem, Oregon

WINTER AND SPRING

HOOK SIZE: 14 to 16, 2XL (Mustad #94831)
THREAD: Brown
TAILS: Dark dun fibers
BODY: Dark brown fur dubbing
WING: Gray duck quill section, set low
HACKLE: Dark dun

Dave reports, "This little dark stonefly is nearly unknown to fishermen in the Pacific Northwest. Only a few rivers are open to trout fishing during early emergence," which he says occurs from January to May in the Coast Range, February to May in the Cascades, and April to June in the High Desert. "There are a few rivers and spring creeks with very cold water where the little dark stonefly does not emerge until late spring," he continues. "Such rivers are the Metolius and Williamson. Both the nymph and the dry fly are worked around fallen trees or brush over the river bank. Because of their small size, these patterns should be cast to feeding fish." This fly is not shown because it is very similar to McNeese's Needlefly, shown in Plate 4.

EARLY BROWN STONEFLY WET (Plate 4)
Matt Vinciguerra, Brewster, New York

STROPHOPTERYX FASCIATA
EARLY SPRING

HOOK SIZE: 16 (Mustad #9672)
THREAD: Black
TAILS: Rusty dun hackle
BODY: Stripped peacock dyed mahogany
WING: Gray duck quill rolled flat
LEGS: Rusty blue dun

NEEDLEFLY (Plate 4)
Dave McNeese, Salem, Oregon

> LEUCTRA ADULT
> EARLY SPRING
>
> HOOK SIZE: 14 to 16, 2XL (Mustad #94831)
> THREAD: Brown
> TAILS: Dark dun fibers
> BODY: Dark brown fur dubbing
> WING: Mottled dark brown turkey
> HACKLE: Dark dun
> (Note: the wing does not overlap the sides of the body.)

McNeese says, "The Brown Bucktail caddis pattern is an excellent fly for *all* little brown stones. Unlike *Taeniopteryx*, the *Nemoura, Leuctra,* and *Capnia* species do exist in fishable populations in many mountain streams in the early part of the trout season. However, most anglers are not familiar with these small stoneflies even when they are in abundance, and it's rare to find commercial ties available."

RED BROWN NYMPH (Plate 4)
Gary Borger, Wausau, Wisconsin

> STROPHOPTERYX FASCIATA
> EARLY SPRING
>
> HOOK SIZE: 10 to 14 (Mustad #9672) and 8 to 14 (Mustad #94840)
> THREAD: Pre-waxed Monocord, size depending on hook size, color to match body
> TAILS: Pheasant tail fibers, dyed to color if necessary
> BODY: Dubbed fur, dark rusty brown, or fuzzy yarns well picked out, weighted
> LEGS: Guard hairs; insert in dubbing loop as for Mono Stonefly Nymph
> WING CASES: Peacock herl pulled tight over top of thorax

This is Borger's version of the Early Brown Stonefly. Gary adds that the nymph can also be tied in medium dark brown, black, light yellow, chartreuse, and gray-brown (such as hare's ear dubbing) to imitate nymphs of the Capniidae, Nemouridae, Chloroperlidae, and Perlodidae families. He cautions, however, that while the light yellow and chartreuse nymphs of the Perlodidae and Chloroperlidae "are productive in early summer when the adults are hatching, the eggs of many species do not hatch until late fall, and so summer and fall fishing with these nymphs is poor at best."

LITTLE BLACK STONEFLY DRY (Plate 2)
Jay Neve, Bellevue, Michigan, and Don Fox, Chassel, Michigan

CAPNIIDAE ADULT

EARLY SPRING

HOOK SIZE: 10 to 18 (Mustad #94833)
TAIL: Black mink tail guard hairs
BODY: Black mink dubbing (from same tail as above)
HACKLE: Black, palmered, dry-fly quality
WINGS: Blackish hen hackle tips, tied three-quarters spent

This fly is intended to be moved while on the water—as are most palmered flies. The 14 to 18 sizes are fished during April and early May to imitate the adult stage of *Paracapnia opis,* formerly *Capnia vernalis.* Peak activity seems to be between 3 and 4 p.m. The 10 and 12 sizes come into use in late June and early July in the lower peninsula and all of July in the upper peninsula to simulate *Acroneuria.* This adult seems most active from 10 p.m. to midnight, with scattered ovipositing throughout the night.

PELTOPERLA NYMPH (Plate 4)
Paul Schmookler, Bronx, New York

SPRING

HOOK SIZE: 12 to 18 (Mustad #94845)
THREAD: Mahogany brown
TAILS: Two mahogany brown pheasant tippets
ABDOMEN: Peacock quill dyed mahogany brown
THORAX: Mahogany brown dubbing, rabbit
WING PADS: Mahogany brown pheasant feather, lacquered

LEGS: Mahogany brown partridge or pheasant fibers
HEAD: Mahogany brown pheasant feather, lacquered

A very effective nymph in the East until early June. Best results in riffles and backwaters with some current, not pools. A good nymph to tie in white.

Using a photocopying process, Paul has also tied his Ultra-Realistic *Acroneuria,* shown in Plate 3.

CALINEURIA CALIFORNICA NYMPH (Plate 3)
Dave McNeese, Salem, Oregon

SPRING TO JULY

HOOK SIZE: 4 to 6 (Mustad #9672)
THREAD: Brown
TAIL: Amber goose quill sections
OVERBODY: Light mottled turkey quill section
UNDERBODY: Amber yellow seal mixed with one-quarter part brown hare's ear
RIBBING: Yellow Monocord
THORAX: Same as underbody
WING CASE: Mottled brown turkey quill sections
LEGS: Mottled brown pheasant rump hackles

CALINEURIA CALIFORNICA ADULT (Plate 2)
Dave McNeese, Salem, Oregon

SPRING TO JULY

HOOK SIZE: 4 to 8 (Mustad #9672)
THREAD: Orange
TAIL: Amber goose quill sections
BODY: Amber/orange dubbing
PALMER: Ginger variant saddle hackle wound over body
WING: Light elk set low over body
FRONT HACKLE: Ginger variant/grizzly mix

McNeese notes that the adult of this species, *Calineuria californica,* emerges from late April to early June in the Coast Range, early May to

June in the Cascades, late May to late June in the High Desert Basin, and early June to July in the Rockies. He adds that "adults seem to prefer evening flights in many areas as long as the temperature does not drop rapidly at sunset. Emergence lasts from 10 to 15 days. In arid river systems, flights may disappear after a few weeks."

HESPEROPERLA PACIFICA NYMPH (Plate 3)
Dave McNeese, Salem, Oregon

SPRING TO JULY

HOOK SIZE: 4 (Mustad #9671)
THREAD: Dark brown
TAIL: Barred brown monofilament.
OVERBODY: Dark brown mottled turkey section
UNDERBODY: Amber/light brown seal mix
THORAX: Same as underbody
WING CASE: Hen pheasant or dark turkey
LEGS: Hen pheasant or brown mottled grouse

HESPEROPERLA PACIFICA ADULT
Dave McNeese, Salem, Oregon

SPRING TO JULY

HOOK SIZE: 4 2XL (Mustad #94831)
THREAD: Brown
TAIL: Brown goose quill sections
BODY: Amber/orange dubbing mixed
PALMER: Medium dun saddle hackle wound over body
WING: Dark elk set low over body
HACKLE: Medium dun saddle hackle

Dave reports that *H. pacifica* "is more numerous statewide in Oregon than *Calineuria californica,* possibly because of its habitat requirements. *H. pacifica* survives well at lower pH levels, from 5.5 and up, while *C. californica* requires a slightly higher pH. *H. pacifica* emergence dates often vary from river to river. In rivers without dams, hatches occur in

June and July. In dammed rivers, hatches can and do occur a few weeks later because the tail waters are cooler."

DELAWARE YELLOW STONEFLY WET (Plate 3)
Matt Vinciguerra, Brewster, New York

SPRING, SUMMER, AND FALL

HOOK SIZE: 10, 3X (Herter #7029)
THREAD: Black Monocord
TAILS: Partridge hackle
BODY: Yellow floss
RIBBING: Black thread
WING: Bronze mallard or widgeon
BEARD: Patridge hackle

Tied on a size 10 hook, this impressionistic fly represents either *Isoperla bilineata* or any number of the Perlidae, such as *Acroneuria* or *Phasganophora.*

CATSKILL CURLER (Plate 1)
Matt Vinciguerra, Brewster, New York

PTERONARCYS OR *ALLONARCYS* SPECIES
SPRING, SUMMER, AND FALL

HOOK SIZE: 6, 6XL (Mustad #9575)
THREAD: Brown Monocord
TAILS: Peccary
BODY: Raw brown wool
WING PADS: Dark brown turkey tail section, Pliobonded, from one piece
LEGS: Hen pheasant tail fibers
HEAD: Turkey tail section

This is Matt's nymph mentioned in chapter 1. Tied on a number 6, 6X hook, it could also represent *Pteronarcella.* This nymph can be used anywhere that any of the above species are found, which means that the imitation can be fished almost anywhere in North America.

MONO STONEFLY NYMPH (Plate 3)
Gary Borger, Wausau, Wisconsin

PTERONARCYIDAE OR PERLIDAE
SPRING AND FALL

HOOK SIZE: 2 to 12 (Mustad #9672)

THREAD: Pre-waxed Monocord, color to match underbody

TAILS: Fibers from leading edge (short side) of goose primary feather, tied one along either side of the hook and spread into a "V" position

FOUNDATION: Lead fuse wire set at sides of hook, extending forward to head

UNDERBODY: Floss, completely covering foundation and lacquered; if body is dark on top, color with felt-tip pen after lacquer has dried

ABDOMEN: Flat monofilament or Swannundaze, clear or only lightly dyed with Rit dye; abdomen should cover rear half of hook shank

THORAX: Dubbed fur or fuzzy yarns, well picked out; white fur mixed in to represent gills

LEGS: Calf tail hair or various guard hairs; form a dubbing loop with tying thread and apply dubbing to one side of loop (if fuzzy yarn is being used, lay it along one side of the loop), insert hair for legs into the loop and at right angles to the thread of the loop, close the loop and spin tight

WING PADS: Dark turkey, pre-lacquered with vinyl head cement to prevent splitting; tie turkey section in at rear of thorax; wind on first half of thorax dubbing; crimp the turkey section so that it extends back over the abdomen a short ways, then fold it forward and tie down at the midpoint of thorax; wind remaining thorax dubbing; crimp the turkey section so that it extends back over the first wing pad a short ways, then fold forward and tie down at head

ANTENNAE (OPTIONAL): Dark turkey fibers set in at sides of head

MOST USED COLORS: All black; abdomen black on top and pale yellow beneath, thorax pale yellow, legs black; abdomen and thorax mottled amber and dark brown

Borger says that "in rocky streams of all sizes, the large nymphs of the families Pteronarcyidae and Perlidae are by far the most significant stonefly fauna in the upper Midwest. The huge black to dark brown nymphs of *Pteronarcys dorsata* and the only slightly smaller *P. pictetii* require 3 years to reach maturity and are thus available as trout food all year long. The Perlidae nymphs vary in color from the dark-backed, pale-bellied *Paragnetina* to the mottled amber *Acroneuria*. The most abundant species require 2 years (and possibly 3 years in some instances) to mature. Thus, like the Pteronarcyidae, these insects serve as trout fodder all year long."

Borger continues: "Resident stream trout feed heavily on these big Pteronarcyidae and Perlidae nymphs, and although the big imitations will take these trout anytime, the nymphs are most effective in spring and fall, before and after the flurry of summer hatches of other insects. In addition, trout which ascend the streams flowing into the Great Lakes during the spring and fall spawning runs will feed on Pteronarcyidae and Perlidae nymphs. A knowledgeable angler can experience some exciting nymph fishing during these runs."

CURVED DORSATA NYMPH (Plate 1)
Jay Neve, Bellevue, Michigan, and Don Fox, Chassel, Michigan

PTERONARCYS DORSATA NYMPH

SPRING AND FALL

HOOK SIZE: 4 to 10 (English bait hooks)

TAILS: Dark brown goose biots

BODY: Two pins tied on sides of hook shank (à la Schwiebert), then wrapped with lead wire (optional), followed by tying thread to shape body, and covering with chocolate brown fur seal overbody

WING PADS: Dark turkey tail (pre-stiffened with Grumbacher's Tuffilm)

LEGS: Dark brown partridge

GILLS: Duck down

ANTENNAE: Dark brown goose biots

"This is now our standard daytime nymph," Neve and Fox say. "It has also proved itself on steelhead the few times we've had the opportunity to fish steelhead."

DON'S BROWN STONEFLY NYMPH (Plate 1)
Jay Neve, Bellevue, Michigan, and Don Fox, Chassel, Michigan

PTERONARCYS DORSATA NYMPH
SPRING AND FALL

HOOK SIZE: 4 to 10 (Mustad #79580)
THREAD: Brown
BODY: Two pins tied on sides of hook shank (à la Schwiebert) and
    wrapped with lead wire, then covered with yellow floss, marked
    with two longitudinal black stripes (with Pantone pen), and
    finally covered with dark brown transparent Swannundaze
WING PADS: Latex or commercial wing material
LEGS: Turkey tail fibers (knotted)
GILLS: Duck down
ANTENNAE: Dark brown goose biots

Fox and Neve say, "We fished this pattern heavily until some striking
successes with the curved, fur-bodied tie we evolved into forced a change.
This is still a standard in our fly boxes, and is a good night pattern fished
with floating line. We use it on nights with a lot of moonlight; bright
moonlit nights seemingly bring less surface activity."

CURVED LYCORIAS NYMPH (Plate 3)
Jay Neve, Bellevue, Michigan, and Don Fox, Chassel, Michigan

ACRONEURIA LYCORIAS NYMPH
SPRING AND FALL

HOOK SIZE: 6 to 12 (English bait hook)
THREAD: Brown
TAILS: Dark brown goose biots
BODY: Two pins tied on sides of hook shank and (optional)
    wrapped with lead wire. Use tying thread to shape the body,
    then cover with yellow mink dubbing segmented with tying
    thread. Darken top of back with dark brown or black Pantone
    pen
WING CASES: Peacock secondary or latex

LEGS: Turkey quill fibers

GILLS: Yellow mink fur, picked

ANTENNAE: Dark brown goose biots, or javelina tips on smaller flies

This is Neve's and Fox's "fish the water" nymph for the Upper Peninsula of Michigan. "We also fish curved versions of mayfly nymphs," they write, "but we have not noticed the decided difference in results that the curved stonefly nymphs afford us."

DON'S MOTTLED STONEFLY NYMPH (Plate 3)
Jay Neve, Bellevue Michigan, and Don Fox, Chassel, Michigan

ACRONEURIA LYCORIAS NYMPH

SPRING AND FALL

HOOK SIZE: 4 to 10 (Mustad #79580)

THREAD: Brown

TAILS: Dark brown goose biots

BODY: Two pins tied on sides of hook shank and wrapped with lead wire. This is covered with yellow floss segmented with black Pantone pen and covered with clear Swannundaze

GILLS: Yellow mink fur, picked

WING CASES: Peacock secondary, or cream latex mottled with black Pantone pen

LEGS: Yellowish turkey tail fibers, knotted

ANTENNAE: Dark brown goose biots

Neve and Fox report: "This pattern imitates *Acroneuria lycorias,* a big major stonefly nymph in most of the fast free-stone streams of the Upper Peninsula of Michigan. We also tie it in size 10 to represent *Isoperla bilineata,* the most numerous of the smaller stoneflies" in the peninsula. "We now fish the 'Curved *Lycorias* Nymph' . . . at most times," admit Neve and Fox, "but this one looks gorgeous in the fly box."

HENWING BOMBER (Plate 2)
Jay Neve, Bellevue, Michigan, and Don Fox, Chassel, Michigan

ACRONEURIA LYCORIAS OR *ISOPERLA BILINEATA* ADULT
SPRING TO JUNE

HOOK SIZE: 6 to 12 (Mustad #94833 or #94840)
THREAD: Gray
TAILS: Dun mink guard tail hairs
BODY: Yellow mink fur and gray-brown muskrat fur, coarsely mixed
HACKLE: Super grizzly palmered on body, and super grizzly and dark brown in front
WINGS: Hen grizzly, tied three-quarters spent

This very "buggy" fly that really doesn't have the wings of a stonefly is fished in May and June to represent *Acroneuria,* which is night-active, and in the smaller size in April to simulate *Isoperla bilineata,* which is often day-active. Neve and Fox have also fished the Henwing Bomber during Michigan's *Hexagenia* hatch with good results. It has also taken fish on remote Canadian lakes during caddis hatches. As Neve and Fox say, "When nothing else works, we tie on a Henwing Bomber and skitter it on the surface."

HAIR WING STONEFLY (Plate 2)
Gary Borger, Wausau, Wisconsin

PTERONARCYIDAE OR PERLIDAE ADULTS
APRIL TO SEPTEMBER

HOOK SIZE: 2 to 12 (Mustad #9672)
THREAD: Pre-waxed Monocord, color to match body
TAIL: Clump of woodchuck guard hairs, tied short
ABDOMEN: Fur chenille clipped to shape. Form a dubbing loop, cut fur from hide and insert in loop at right angles to thread of loop, close loop and spin tight
THORAX: Dubbed fur

LEGS: Good quality, dry-fly hackle wound over thorax and head and trimmed top and bottom; use two hackle feathers each for thorax and head

HEAD: Dubbed fur

WING: Clump of woodchuck hair with underfur left in; tie in just ahead of thorax

(MOST USED BODY COLORS: Pale yellow and black mottled; pale yellow and tan)

Borger says, "Pteronarcyidae emerge and lay eggs during the dark hours. Pteronarcyidae adults are on the wing in the upper Midwest from late April to the first of July; the heaviest flights occur around the first of June. An adult imitation is a deadly night pattern during this time," he adds. "On some streams, the hatch is so heavy that insects are on the water even during the daytime. These flights rival the hatches of the huge Western species for angling excitement. The tan to amber adults of Perlidae emerge from May to September, with the heaviest flights occurring in June," Borger explains. "Like the Pteronarcyidae, these big adults provide superb night fishing."

PTERONARCYS CALIFORNICA NYMPH (Plate 1)
Dave McNeese, Salem, Oregon

LATE APRIL TO MID-JUNE

HOOK SIZE: 4 to 10 (Mustad #9575)
THREAD: Black
TAILS: Mottled monofilament
OVERBODY: Dark brown mottled turkey section
UNDERBODY: Black/brown seal mixed
RIBBING: 4-pound-test brown monofilament
THORAX: Black/brown/orange seal mixed
WING CASE: Dark brown turkey or goose quill section
LEGS: Blackish hen cape feather

PTERONARCYS CALIFORNICA ADULT (Plate 2)
Dave McNeese, Salem, Oregon

LATE APRIL TO MID-JUNE

HOOK SIZE: 4 to 8 (Mustad #9575)
THREAD: Orange
TAIL: Brown goose quill section
BODY: Black/brown/orange mixed dubbing
PALMER: Dark blue dun saddle hackle wound over body
WING: Dark elk, set low over body
FRONT HACKLE: Dark blue dun saddle hackle

Dave notes that *P. californica* emerges from late April to early June in the Coast Range, March to mid-May in the Cascade Range, mid-May to mid-June in the High Desert Basin, and late May to July in the Rockies. After emergence, says Dave, a small stonefly nymph is effective. "My best is a Montana nymph," he reports. "The fish prefer a much smaller fly late in the season, as the large nymphs have emerged in early summer."

POLAR COMMANDER (Plate 2)
Jay Neve, Bellevue, Michigan, and Don Fox, Chassel, Michigan

PTERONARCYS DORSATA ADULT
MAY TO JUNE

HOOK SIZE: 2 to 10 (Mustad #9672 or #79580)
THREAD: Yellow
TAILS: Widely forked ginger goose biots
BODY: Yellow deer hair tied parallel to shank and wrapped with
   brown rod-winding thread to secure and sectionalize body
WING: Polar bear (or white bucktail or calftail)
HACKLE: Mixed grizzly and dark brown/or grizzly to rear and dark
   brown in front

Neve and Fox say, "This fly has caught more large fish for us than any other fly. It is our basic night fly. We have tried this same fly with brown deer hair wrapped with yellow rod-winding thread and have had equal success. *Pteronarcys dorsata's* habit of ovipositing in the early morning and the resulting heavy strikes made us go to heavy hooks to help in hooking and landing larger fish," they explain. "We have caught more than 20 fish on one fly before being forced to change."

ISOPERLA FULVA NYMPH (Plate 4)
Dave McNeese, Salem, Oregon

MID-MAY TO AUGUST

HOOK SIZE: 10 to 14 (Mustad #9671)
THREAD: Yellow
TAIL: Wood duck fibers
OVERBODY: Wood duck section
UNDERBODY: Yellowish fur dubbing
RIBBING: Yellow thread
THORAX: Same as underbody
WING CASE: Wood duck section
LEGS: Wood duck fibers

ISOPERLA FULVA ADULT (Plate 4)
Dave McNeese, Salem, Oregon

MID-MAY TO AUGUST

HOOK SIZE: 10 to 12 (Mustad #94840)
THREAD: Yellow
TAILS: Yellow goose quill sections
BODY: Yellow fur dubbing
WING: Light gray deer hair, topped with mallard quill section
PARACHUTE HACKLE: Light blue dun or grizzly

This parachute-style yellow stonefly is tied to simulate the very low profile of the adult on the surface of the water. "Movement on the surface is less active than caddis, with minimal running movement across the surface," says McNeese.

This is the most common Western *Isoperla,* and has been found in a wide range of habitats. Its emergence is from June to early July in the Coast Range, and from late June to August from the Cascades to the Rockies.

MONTY'S GOLDEN STONE (Plate 3)
R. "Monty" Montplaisir, Colebrook, New Hampshire

PHASGANOPHORA CAPITATA NYMPH

JUNE, JULY, AND SEPTEMBER

HOOK SIZE: 4 (Mustad #9671, bent downward)

THREAD: Black 6/0

TAILS: 4-pound-test monofilament colored with brown Pantone marker

ANTENNAE: Same as tails

UNDERBODY: Loop of 3-amp fuse wire ribbed with .016 lead wire

RIBBING: 4-pound-test monofilament

ABDOMEN: Gold Crafts Fur or Seal-Ex (Crafts Fur, a synthetic, resembles seal fur, but its long fibers dub to thread more easily)

OVERBODY: Chicken-feed bag strips colored with brown Pantone marker

WING CASE: Same as overbody

THORAX: Gold Crafts Fur or Seal-Ex

LEGS: Gold Dazzle-Aire yarn colored with brown Pantone marker (Dazzle-Aire, four-ply knitting yarn, comes in a variety of solid colors with flecks of metallic silver interwoven in each strand. It is made by Caron International, Inc., and can be purchased in discount department stores)

LITTLE YELLOW ADULT, WITH EGG SAC (Plate 4)
Dave McNeese, Salem, Oregon

JUNE TO AUGUST

HOOK SIZE: 12 to 16 (Mustad #94840)

THREAD: Yellow

TAILS: Light dun fibers

EGG SAC: Short section of fluorescent orange floss tied under tail

REAR HACKLE: Light dun

BODY: Yellow fur dubbing

FRONT HACKLE: Light dun

The little yellow stoneflies emerge from mid-June into August. Cold headwaters have a July and August emergence.

APPENDIX:

EMERGENCE TABLES

TABLE 1
SEASONAL SUCCESSION AND DIVERSITY OF STONEFLIES ON A MASSACHUSETTS STREAM

From "Seasonal Succession and Diversity of Stoneflies (Plecoptera) in Factory Brook, Massachusetts," by Richard J. Neves, *Journal of the New York Entomological Society*, Vol. 36 No. 3, 1978

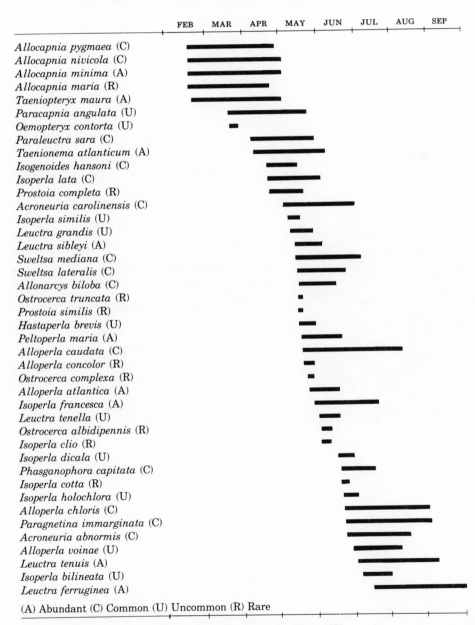

(A) Abundant (C) Common (U) Uncommon (R) Rare

Seasonal occurrence of adult Plecoptera along Factory Brook, 1974 to 1976.

TABLE 2
STONEFLY EMERGENCE IN TERREBONNE
COUNTY, QUEBEC

From "Cycles vitaux de quelques Plécoptères des
Laurentides (insectes)" by Peter Harper and Etienne
Magnin, *Canadian Journal of Zoology,* Vol. 47, No. 4, 1969

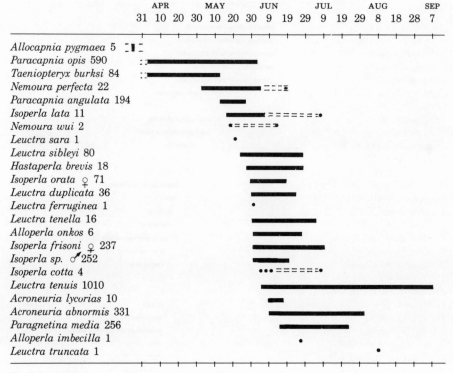

The figures indicate the number of specimens collected.

TABLE 3
EMERGENCE PATTERNS OF STONEFLIES IN A WISCONSIN CREEK

Adapted from information in "Emergence Pattern of Stoneflies (Plecoptera) in Otter Creek, Wisconsin," by Richard P. Narf and William L. Hilsenhoff, *The Great Lakes Entomologist,* Vol. 7, No. 4, 1974

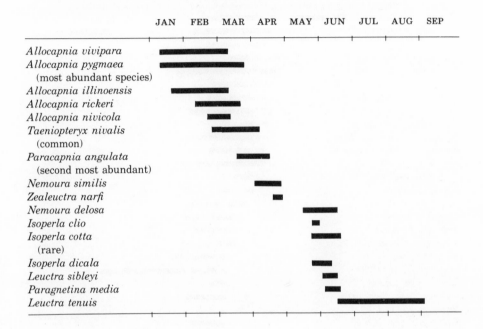

	JAN	FEB	MAR	APR	MAY	JUN	JUL	AUG	SEP

Allocapnia vivipara
Allocapnia pygmaea
  (most abundant species)
Allocapnia illinoensis
Allocapnia rickeri
Allocapnia nivicola
Taeniopteryx nivalis
  (common)
Paracapnia angulata
  (second most abundant)
Nemoura similis
Zealeuctra narfi
Nemoura delosa
Isoperla clio
Isoperla cotta
  (rare)
Isoperla dicala
Leuctra sibleyi
Paragnetina media
Leuctra tenuis

TABLE 4
STONEFLY EMERGENCE PATTERNS ON AN OREGON STREAM
From "Emergence Patterns of Plecoptera in a Stream in Oregon, USA," by
Cary D. Kerst and N. H. Anderson, *Freshwater Biology,* Vol. 4, 1974

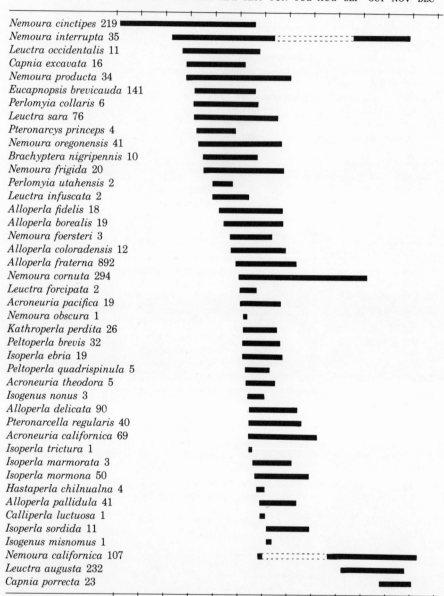

DEC JAN FEB MAR APR MAY JUN JUL AUG SEP OCT NOV DEC

Nemoura cinctipes 219
Nemoura interrupta 35
Leuctra occidentalis 11
Capnia excavata 16
Nemoura producta 34
Eucapnopsis brevicauda 141
Perlomyia collaris 6
Leuctra sara 76
Pteronarcys princeps 4
Nemoura oregonensis 41
Brachyptera nigripennis 10
Nemoura frigida 20
Perlomyia utahensis 2
Leuctra infuscata 2
Alloperla fidelis 18
Alloperla borealis 19
Nemoura foersteri 3
Alloperla coloradensis 12
Alloperla fraterna 892
Nemoura cornuta 294
Leuctra forcipata 2
Acroneuria pacifica 19
Nemoura obscura 1
Kathroperla perdita 26
Peltoperla brevis 32
Isoperla ebria 19
Peltoperla quadrispinula 5
Acroneuria theodora 5
Isogenus nonus 3
Alloperla delicata 90
Pteronarcella regularis 40
Acroneuria californica 69
Isoperla trictura 1
Isoperla marmorata 3
Isoperla mormona 50
Hastaperla chilnualna 4
Alloperla pallidula 41
Calliperla luctuosa 1
Isoperla sordida 11
Isogenus misnomus 1
Nemoura californica 107
Leuctra augusta 232
Capnia porrecta 23

Based on collections from 31 months from Oak Creek, Benton Co., Oregon.

TABLE 5
SEASONAL DISTRIBUTION OF STONEFLIES, WESTERN UNITED STATES.

From "The Stoneflies (Plecoptera) of Montana," by Arden R. Gaufin, William E. Ricker, Michael Miner, Paul Milam and Richard A. Hays, *Transactions of the American Entomological Society,* Vol. 98, 1972

JAN FEB MAR APR MAY JUN JUL AUG SEP OCT NOV DEC

Peltoperla brevis
Peltoperla mariana
Nemoura banksi
Nemoura venusta
Nemoura tumana
Nemoura californica
Nemoura coloradensis
Nemoura flexura
Nemoura tina
Nemoura decepta
Nemoura delicatula
Nemoura besametsa
Nemoura nevadensis interrupta
Nemoura cataractae
Nemoura cinctipes
Nemoura columbiana
Nemoura cordillera
Nemoura frigida
Nemoura glacier
Nemoura haysi
Nemoura oregonensis
Leuctra augusta
Leuctra forcipata
Leuctra occidentalis
Leuctra purcellana
Leuctra sara
Paraleuctra jewetti
Paraleuctra rickeri
Perlomyia collaris
Perlomyia utahensis
Megaleuctra stigmata
Capnia confusa
Capnia coloradensis
Capnia elongata
Capnia gracilaria
Capnia limata
Capnia nana
Capnia oenone
Capnia petila
Capnia sextuberculata

TABLE 5
SEASONAL DISTRIBUTION OF STONEFLIES,
WESTERN UNITED STATES *(continued)*

JAN FEB MAR APR MAY JUN JUL AUG SEP OCT NOV DEC

Capnia projecta
Capnia milami
Capnia sasquatchi
Capnia spenceri
Capnia columbiana
Capnia distincta
Capnia poda
Capnia trava
Eucapnopsis brevicauda
Eucapnopsis vedderensis
Isocapnia crinita
Isocapnia grandis
Isocapnia hyalita
Isocapnia missourii
Isocapnia vedderensis
Brachyptera occidentalis
Brachyptera nigripennis
Brachyptera pacifica
Brachyptera pallida
Pteronarcella badia
Pteronarcella regularis
Pteronarcys californica
Pteronarcys dorsata
Arcynopteryx compacta
Arcynopteryx signata
Arcynopteryx subtruncata
Arcynopteryx watertoni
Arcynopteryx aurea
Arcynopteryx bradleyi
Arcynopteryx parallela
Arcynopteryx curvata
Isogenus aestivalis
Isogenus pilatus
Isogenus tostonus
Isogenus elongatus
Isogenus expansus
Isogenus frontalis
  colubrinus
Isogenus modestus
Isogenus nonus
Isoperla ebria
Isoperla fulva
Isoperla fusca
Isoperla longiseta

TABLE 5
SEASONAL DISTRIBUTION OF STONEFLIES,
WESTERN UNITED STATES *(continued)*

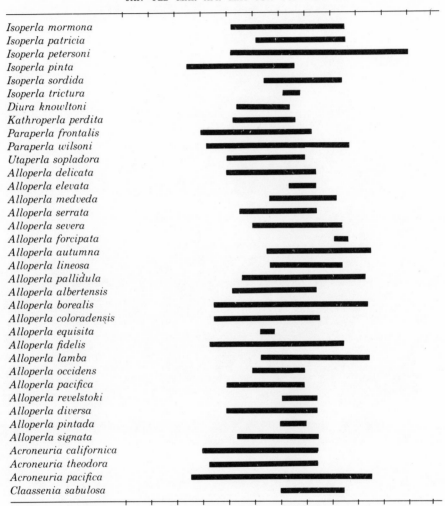

	JAN	FEB	MAR	APR	MAY	JUN	JUL	AUG	SEP	OCT	NOV	DEC

Isoperla mormona
Isoperla patricia
Isoperla petersoni
Isoperla pinta
Isoperla sordida
Isoperla trictura
Diura knowltoni
Kathroperla perdita
Paraperla frontalis
Paraperla wilsoni
Utaperla sopladora
Alloperla delicata
Alloperla elevata
Alloperla medveda
Alloperla serrata
Alloperla severa
Alloperla forcipata
Alloperla autumna
Alloperla lineosa
Alloperla pallidula
Alloperla albertensis
Alloperla borealis
Alloperla coloradensis
Alloperla equisita
Alloperla fidelis
Alloperla lamba
Alloperla occidens
Alloperla pacifica
Alloperla revelstoki
Alloperla diversa
Alloperla pintada
Alloperla signata
Acroneuria californica
Acroneuria theodora
Acroneuria pacifica
Claassenia sabulosa

BIBLIOGRAPHY

Pending completion of the *Nymphs of North American Stonefly Genera* by Kenneth W. Stewart and Bill P. Stark, which will probably see publication circa 1986, anglers interested in North American stoneflies should consult Peter W. Claassen's *Plecoptera Nymphs of America (North of Mexico)* (Charles C Thomas, Springfield, Illinois, and Baltimore, 1931), and J. G. Needham and P. W. Claassen's *A Monograph of the Plecoptera or Stoneflies of America North of Mexico* (the Entomological Society of America, Lafayette, Indiana, 1925), reprinted without change by the Entomological Society of America in 1970. Claassen's *A Catalogue of the Plecoptera of the World* (Cornell University Agricultural Experiment Station, Ithaca, New York, 1939) has been superseded by J. Illies, "Katalog der Rezenten Plecoptera," in *Das Tierreich*, Volume 82, 1966, which is most helpful in giving the geographical locales for individual stonefly species, and Peter Zwick's "Insecta: Plecoptera, Phylogenetisches System und Katalog," in *Das Tierreich*, Volume 94, 1973, a whopper at $200 a copy.

An excellent summary of stoneflies worldwide is to be had in H. B. N. Hynes's "Biology of Plecoptera" in the *Annual Review of Entomology*, Volume 21, 1976. A stimulating discussion is also provided in Hynes's "The Stream and Its Valley," *Verh. Internat. Verein. Limnol.*, Volume 19, October 1975, which deals in part with organic matter in streams and the role of detritovores. Hynes is also the author of a valuable pioneering work, "The Taxonomy and Ecology of the Nymphs of British Plecoptera with Notes on the Adults and Eggs," in the *Transactions of the Royal Entomological Society*, Volume 91, 1941, and a superb book, *The Ecology of Running Waters* (University of Toronto Press, Toronto, 1970), a comprehensive and critical review of the world literature on the biology of streams and rivers. The bibliography alone contains more than 1,500 entries. Another valuable work for the angler gone ga-ga is Per Brinck's "Studies on Swedish Stoneflies," in *Opuscula Entomologica*, Supplement 11, 1949.

In this country, Stephen W. Hitchcock offers an excellent review of stoneflies in the introductory chapter of *The Plecoptera or Stoneflies of Connecticut*, Bulletin 107, State Geological and Natural History Survey of Connecticut, 1974. Hitchcock's study also serves as the best up-to-date reference for the stoneflies of the northeastern United States, with keys to the species level. Other studies for the angler seeking to identify stoneflies of a given region are the following works, given chronologically:

Theodore H. Frison, *Fall and Winter Stoneflies, or Plecoptera, of Illinois*, Bulletin, Division of the [Illinois] Natural History Survey, Volume 18, Article 2, 1929. This was the study that kicked off Frison's interest in stoneflies in general. For an account of its importance, see *A Century of Biological Research,* Bulletin of the Illinois Natural History Survey, Volume 27, Article 2, 1958, see pages 139 to 140. Frison also wrote *The Stoneflies, or Plecoptera, of Illinois,* Bulletin, Division of the [Illinois] Natural History Survey, Volume 20, Article 4, 1935, and *Studies of North American Plecoptera,* Bulletin of the Illinois Natural History Survey, Volume 22, Article 2, 1942.

William E. Ricker, *Stoneflies of Southwestern British Columbia* (Indiana University Publications, Bloomington, Indiana, 1943). Ricker is also the author of *Systematic Studies in Plecoptera* (Indiana University Publications, Bloomington, 1952), and of more than 150 articles and scientific papers. Now in retirement from the Fisheries Research Board of Canada, Ricker possesses a remarkable intellect. Among fishery scientists, he is renowned for his work on population dynamics, including those of the sockeye salmon run on the Fraser River in British Columbia, and of the Peruvian anchovy. Indeed, Ricker is such a commanding authority on both fishes and stoneflies that there are scientists staggered to learn that Ricker, the fish man, and Ricker, the stonefly systematist, are one and the same. Other works by Ricker that may be of interest to the angler are "Distribution of Canadian Stoneflies," in *Gewässer und Abwässer,* Number 34/35, 1964, which includes a history of research on stoneflies; "Distribution of Quebec Stoneflies (Plecoptera)," in *Le Naturaliste Canadien,* Volume 95, 1968; and *The Classification, Evolution and Dispersal of the Winter Stonefly Genus,* ALLOCAPNIA (University of Illinois Press, Urbana, 1971), written with Herbert H. Ross; *Russian-English Dictionary for Students of Fisheries and Aquatic Biology,* Bulletin of the Fisheries Research Board of Canada, 183, 1973; "An Annotated Checklist of the Plecoptera (Insecta) of British Columbia," in *Syesis,* Volume 8, 1975, written with G. E. Scudder; and "Origin of Stonefly Names proposed by Ricker and Collaborators," in *Perla,* Number 2, 1976.

Philip E. Harden and Clarence E. Mickel, *The Stoneflies of Minnesota (Plecoptera),* Technical Bulletin 101, University of Minnesota Agricultural Experiment Station, 1952.

Stanley G. Jewett, Jr., *The Stoneflies of the Pacific Northwest,* Oregon State Monogographs, Studies in Entomology, 3, 1959, and "The Stoneflies (Plecoptera) of California," *Bulletin of the California Insect Survey,* Volume 6, Number 6, 1960.

Arden R. Gaufin, Alan V. Nebeker, and Joann Sessions, *The Stoneflies (Plecoptera) of Utah,* University of Utah Biological Series, Volume 14, Number 1, 1966. Gaufin is also the author of the paper "Environmental Requirements of Plecoptera," in *Biological Problems in Water Pollution,* Third Seminar, August 13 to 17, 1962. Washington, D.C., U. S. Department of Health, Education and Welfare, Public Health Service Publication No. 999-WP-25.

Peter Harper and Etienne Magnin, "Cycles vitaux de quelques Plécoptères des Laurentides (insectes)," in *Canadian Journal of Zoology,* Volume 47, Number 4, 1969.

Arden R. Gaufin, William E. Ricker, Michael Miner, Paul Milam and Richard A. Hays, "The Stoneflies (Plecoptera) of Montana," *Transactions of the American Entomological Society,* Volume 98, 1972.

Cary D. Kerst and N. H. Anderson, "Emergence Patterns of Plecoptera in a Stream in Oregon, USA," in *Freshwater Biology,* Volume 4, 1974, and Kerst and Anderson's, "The Plecoptera Community of a Small Stream in Oregon, USA," in *Freshwater Biology,* Volume 5, 1975.

Richard P. Narf and William L. Hilsenhoff, "Emergence Pattern of Stoneflies (Plecoptera) in Otter Creek, Wisconsin," *The Great Lakes Entomologist,* Volume 7, Number 4, 1974.

See also Hilsenhoff's, *Aquatic Insects of Wisconsin,* Technical Bulletin 89, Department of Natural Resources, Madison, Wisconsin, 1975.

Rebecca F. Surdick and Ke Chung Kim, *Stoneflies (Plecoptera) of Pennsylvania,* Bulletin 808, The Pennsylvania State University College of Agriculture, 1976.

Richard W. Baumann, Arden R. Gaufin, and Rebecca F. Surdick, *The Stoneflies (Plecoptera) of the Rocky Mountains,* Memoirs of the American Entomological Society, Number 31, 1977.

Richard J. Neves, "Seasonal Succession and Diversity of Stoneflies (Plecoptera) in Factory Brook, Massachusetts," *Journal of the New York Entomological Society,* Volume 86, Number 3, 1978.

Stanley W. Szczytko and Kenneth W. Stewart, "The Stoneflies (Plecoptera) of Texas," *Transactions of the American Entomological Society,* Volume 103, 1977, and *The Genus* ISOPERLA *(Plecoptera) of Western North America: Holomorphology and Systematics, and a New Stonefly Genus* CASCADOPERLA, Memoirs of the American Entomological Society, Number 32, 1979.

Stewart is the co-author of several life histories of Plecoptera species, such as George L. Vaught and Stewart, "The Life History and Ecology of the Stonefly *Neoperla clymene* (Newman) (Plecoptera: Perlidae)," in the *Annals of the Entomological Society of America,* Volume 67, Number 2, 1974; Reed Y. Orbendorfer and Stewart, "The Life Cycle of *Hydroperla crosbyi* (Plecoptera: Perlodidae),"*Great Basin Naturalist,* Volume 37, Number 2, 1977; Rosalyn K. Snellen and Stewart, "The Life Cycle of *Perlesta placida* (Plecoptera: Perlidae) in an Intermittent Stream in Northern Texas," *Annals of the Entomological Society of America,* Volume 72, Number 5, 1979; Rosalyn K. Snellen and Stewart, "The Life Cycle and Drumming Behavior of *Zealeuctra claasseni* (Frison) and *Zealeuctra hitei* (Ricker and Ross) (Plecoptera: Leuctridae) in Texas," *Aquatic Insects,* Volume 1, Number 2, 1979.

Other life histories of the Plecoptera include Chenfu Francis Wu, *Morphology, Anatomy and Ethology of Nemoura,* Bulletin of the Lloyd Library of Botany, Natural History, Pharmacy and Materia Medica, Entomological Series Number 3, 1923; D. C. Tarter and L. A. Krumholz, "Life History and Ecology of *Paragnetina media* (Walker) in Doe Run, Meade County, Kentucky," *The American Midland Naturalist,* Volume 86, 1971; Mary R. Cather and Arden F. Gaufin, "Life History and Ecology of *Megarcys signata* (Plecoptera: Perlodidae), Mill Creek, Wasatch Mountains, Utah," *Great Basin Naturalist,* Volume 35, 1975; J. W. Elwood and R. M. Cushman, "The Life History and Ecology of *Peltoperla maria* (Plecoptera: Peltoperlidae) in a Small Spring-fed Stream," *Verh. Internat. Verein. Limnol.,* Volume 19, 1975; P. P. Harper, "Life Histories of Nemouridae and Leuctridae in Southern Ontario (Plecoptera)," *Hydrobiologia,* Volume 41, 1973; D. L. Ashley, D. C. Tarter, and W. C. Watkins, "Life History and Ecology of *Diploperla robusta* (Stark and Gaufin) (Plecoptera: Perlodidae)," *Psyche:* Volume 83, 1976; R. M. Cushman, J. W. Elwood and S. G. Hildebrand, "Life History and Production Dynamics of *Alloperla mediana* and *Diplectona modesta* in Walker Branch, Tennessee," *The American Midland Naturalist,* Volume 98, 1977; C. A. Siegfried and A. W. Knight, "Aspects of the Life History and Growth of *Acroneuria (Calineuria) californica* in a Sierra Foothill Stream," *Annals of the Entomological Society of America,* Volume 71, 1978.

On the food of stoneflies, see Jay W. Richardson and Arden R. Gaufin, "Food Habits of Some Western Stonefly Nymphs," *Transactions of the American Entomological Society,* Volume 97, 1971; Randall L. Fuller and Kenneth W. Stewart, "The Food Habits of Stoneflies (Plecoptera) in the Upper Gunnison River, Colorado," *Environmental Entomology,* Volume

6, Number 2, 1977; "Stonefly (Plecoptera) Food Habits and Prey Preference in the Dolores River, Colorado," *The American Midland Naturalist,* Volume 101, Number 1, 1979; W. P. Kovalak, "On the Feeding Habits of *Phasganophora capitata* (Plecoptera: Perlidae)," *Great Lakes Entomology,* Volume 11, 1978; E. Claire and R. Phillips, "The Stonefly *Acroneuria pacifica* as a Potential Predator on Salmonid Embryos," *Transactions of the American Fisheries Society,* Volume 97, 1968.

For stoneflies and other invertebrates feeding on leaves and other dead organic matter, see D. W. Chapman and R. Demory, "Seasonal Changes in the Food Ingested by Aquatic Insect Larvae and Nymphs in Two Oregon Streams," *Ecology,* Volume 44, 1963, and Chapman, "The Relative Contribution of Aquatic and Terrestrial Primary Producers to the Trophic Relations of Stream Organisms," Special Publications of the Pymatuning Laboratory of Field Biology, Volume 4, 1966; W. F. McDiffett, "The Transformation of Energy by a Stream Detritovore, *Pteronarcys scotti* (Plecoptera)," *Ecology,* Volume 51, 1970; N. K. Kaushik and H. B. N. Hynes, "The Fate of the Dead Leaves That Fall Into Streams," *Archives of Hydrobiology*, Volume 68, 1971; K. W. Cummins, et al.; "The Utilization of Leaf Litter by Stream Detritovores," *Ecology*, Volume 54, 1973; E. F. Benfield, D. S. Jones, M. F. Patterson, "Leaf Pack Processing in a Pastureland Stream," *Oikos*, Volume 29, 1977; N. H. Anderson, "Detritus Processing by Macroinvertebrates in Stream Ecosystems," *Annual Review of Entomology,* 1979; Richard J. Neves, "Secondary Production of Epilithic Fauna in a Woodland Stream," *The American Midland Naturalist,* Volume 102, Number 2, 1979.

The literature on behavioral drift has been growing at an incredible rate. The key references we have used are Paul R. Needham, *Trout Streams,* revised by Carl F. Bond (New York, 1969), Hikaru Tanaka, "On the Daily Change of the Drifting of Benthic Animals in Stream, Especially on the Types of Daily Change Observed in Taxonomic Groups of Insects" (in Japanese, with English summary), *Bulletin of the Freshwater Fishery Research Laboratory, Tokyo,* Volume 9, 1960. Thomas F. Waters, "Diurnal Periodicity in the Drift of Stream Invertebrates,"*Ecology*, Volume 43, Number 2, 1962; Waters, "Interpretation of Invertebrate Drift in Streams," *Ecology,* Volume 46, Number 3, 1965; Waters, "Diurnal Periodicity in the Drift of Day-Active Stream Invertebrates," *Ecology,* Volume 49, Number 1, 1968; Waters, "Diel Patterns of Aquatic Invertebrate Drift in Streams of Northern Utah," *Utah Academy Proceedings,* Volume 46, Part 2, 1969 (from which we have taken Figure 1 in Chapter 2); and Waters, "The Drift of Stream Insects," *Annual Review of Entomology,* 1972. See also N. H. Anderson, "Depressant Effect of Moonlight on Activity of Aquatic Insects," *Nature,* Volume 209, 1966; Charles S. Holt and T. F. Waters, "Effect of Light Intensity on the Drift of Stream Invertebrates," *Ecology,* Volume 48, Number 2, 1967; J. M. Elliott, "Diel Changes in Invertebrate Drift and the Food of Trout," *Journal of Fish Biology,* Volume 2, 1970; Thomas J. Cloud, Jr., and Kenneth W. Stewart, "The Drift of Mayflies (Ephemeroptera) in the Brazos River, Texas," *Journal of the Kansas Entomological Society*, Volume 47, Number 3, 1974; J. David Allan, "Trout Predation and the Size Composition of Stream Drift," *Journal of Limnology and Oceanography,* Volume 23, Number 6, 1978.

INDEX

abdomen of imitation nymph, 52–5
Acroneuria, 27
 habits and behavior, 101–102
 molting, *illus.* 101
 Paul Schmookler's Ultra-Realistic, 6,
  136; standard patterns, 58–63, *illus.*
  60–2, 135; Bill Simpson's, 64–8, *illus.*
  65–8; inverted, 63–4, *illus.* 63
Acroneuria lycorias
 adult (imitation), pattern, 143
 nymph (imitation), pattern, 141–2
adult stonefly, *see* patterns for imitation
  adult stoneflies; stonefly adult,
  imitation; *also* adult *under*
  individual families, genera and
  species
Alabaster Nymph fly, 104–105
Alaska, 5, 36
Allan, J. David, 18–19, 164
Allocapnia, emergence dates, 6
Allocapnia maria, 23
Allocapnia pygmaea, 23
Allonarcys
 habitat, 94
 morphology, 39
 nymph (artificial), pattern, 138
Allonarcys biloba, 39
 adult, 127
 nymph, 5, illus. 38, 88
Allonarcys comstocki, 39
Allonarcys proteus, 39
Allonarcys scotti, 39

Alloperla, nymph, 32–3
Anderson, Norman H., 15, 154, 162, 164
antennae, artificial, 57
Aquatic Insects (periodical), 12
artificial adult stonefly, *see* patterns for
  imitation adult stoneflies; stonefly
  adult, imitation
artificial nymph, *see* patterns for
  imitation nymphs; stonefly nymph,
  imitation
Ashley, D. L., 163
Ausable River, east branch, New York,
  103–104
Au Sable River, south branch, Michigan,
  125, 126

Babers, Frank H., 100
Baetis (mayfly), behavioral drift, 17, 18
bass, striped, 5
Baumann, Richard W., 12, 24, 163
behavioral drift, 14–18, *illus.* 16
 of *Alloperla,* 33
 bibliography, 164
 and fishing technique, 85–9
"belly" in line, 81–2, 92
Benfield, E. F., 13, 164
big golden stones, *see* Perlidae
Black Woolly Bug pattern, 75, *illus.* 74
Black Woolly Worm pattern, 73–5, *illus.*
  74
boat fishing, *see* float fishing

Borger, Gary, 116
  fly patterns of, 131–2, 134–5, 139–40,
    143–4
Brinck, Per, 161
Brooks, Charles E.
  Alabaster Nymph fly, 104–105
  on K's Butt Salmonfly, 108
  Montana Stone pattern, 68–9
  on *P. californica* nymph, 36–7
  Salmonfly pattern for *P. Californica*,
    121
Brown Woolly Worm pattern, 74–5

Calineuria californica
  adult (imitation), pattern, 136–7
  hatch, 27
  nymph: behavioral drift, 17; imitation,
    pattern, 136
Cameron, Angus, 92, 103–104
Cape Cod Woolly (Black Woolly Bug)
  pattern, 75, *illus.* 74
Capnia lacustra, adult, 11
Capnia vernalis, see *Paracapnia opis*
Capniidae, 23–4
  adult (imitation), patterns, 131–2
    135
casting technique
  in "big waters," 92
  while boat fishing, *illus.* 95, 96
  interrupted, 92, *illus.* 93
  of Ted Niemeyer, 88–9, *illus.* 89
  nymphs, 84–5
  twitching method, 124, 126
  upstream hold cast, 82, *illus.* 83, 124,
    127
  wet-fly (of M. Montplaisir), 87–8, *illus.*
    87
Cather, Mary R., 163
Catskill Curler pattern, 138
Chapman, D. W., 164
chenille, as abdominal material, 54
Chloroperlidae, 32–3
  adult (imitation), pattern, 131–2
  habitat, 77–8
Claassen, Peter W., 12, 161
Claassenia sabulosa, 29
  nymph: food and predation, 28–9;
    imitation, pattern, 130–1
Claire, Errol W., 27, 164
Cloud, Thomas J., Jr., 17, 164
color-coding artificial flies, 51
Cooper, Don, 100

Croton River, lower, New York, 5,
  100–101
Cummins, K. W., 164
Curved *dorsata* nymph pattern, 140
Curved *lycorias* nymph pattern, 141–2
Cushman, R. M., 163

Delaware Yellow Stonefly Wet pattern,
  138
Demory, R., 164
detritovorous stoneflies, 13–14
  bibliography, 164
  Nemouridae, 24
diapause (arrested development), 11
Don's Brown Stonefly Nymph pattern,
  141
Don's Mottled Stonefly Nymph pattern,
  142
Draper, Keith, 51
drift, *see* behavioral drift
drumming signals, 10
dry stonefly
  fishing, 121–7
  tying, 107–21
  see also patterns for imitation adult
    stoneflies

Early Brown Stonefly Wet pattern, 133
"Early Brown Stones," *see*
  Taeniopterygidae
eggs of stoneflies, depositing and
  hatching, 11
Elliott, J. M., 18, 164
Elwood, J. W., 163
emergence
  and fishing techniques, 85, 123–4
  of salmonfly *(P. californica),* 3–4, 38,
    121–2
emergence dates, 6, 123; tables, 151–7
  of *Allonarcys* species, 39
  of *A. pygmaea,* 23
  of *C. californica,* 136–7
  of *C. sabulosa,* 29
  of *I. bilineata,* 33
  of *I. fulva,* 34–5
  of *N. clymene,* 29
  of *P. badia,* 36
  of *P. californica,* 36, 38
  of *P. maria,* 36
  of *P. media,* 32

emergence dates *(continued)*
  of *P. placida,* 30
  of *P. princeps,* 38
  of *S. fasciata,* 26
  of *S. vallicularia,* 25
  tables, regional: Massachusetts (table
    1), 151; Oregon (table 4), 154;
    Quebec (table 2), 152; Western U.S.
    (table 5), 155; Wisconsin
    (table 3), 153
  of *T. nivalis,* 27
  of *Z. claasseni,* 23
equipment
  leader, 84, 91, 126
  line, 79–81, 91, 95
  reel, 79
  rod, 78–9, 91, 95, 123, 127
Esopus Creek, New York, 5, 88
Euholognatha, 22–7, *illus.* 22
eyes, artificial, 58

feather(s)
  biots, as tail material, 51
  fibers, as leg material, 57
  as wing cases or pads, 56–7, *illus.* 56
  see also quill butts; quill sheathing
fishing techniques
  casting, *see* casting technique
  for dry stonefly, 121–7
  float fishing, 94–6, illus. 95
  mending line, 81–3, *illus.* 81, 92
  night fishing, 124–6
  for nymphs, 77–8, 81–3, 84–97
  points to remember (list), 96–7
  in runs and pockets, 90–1
  for small streams, 93–4, 126–7
flat-bodied nymph, imitation, 45–6, *illus.*
    45
flat oval-shaped nymph, imitation, 48
    and *illus.*
Flick, Art, 26
floatability of artificial adult stonefly, 107
float fishing, 94–6, *illus.* 95
floss, woven, as abdominal material, 52
fly tying
  adults, patterns, *see* patterns for
    imitation adult stoneflies
  color-coding, 51
  floatability, 107
  nymphs, 43–75; materials, 44–58;
    patterns, *see* patterns for imitation

nymphs; weighting, 44–51; white,
    100
  realism of, 43–4, 55
food of stoneflies, 13
  bibliography, 163–4
Fothergill, Chuck, 78, 91
Fox, Don, and Jay Neve, fly patterns of,
    131, 135, 140, 141–2, 143, 145–6
Franklin, D. R., 17
Frison, Theodore H., 12, 24, 33, 161–2
Fuller, Randall L., 28–9, 34, 36, 163
fur
  as abdominal material, 54
  as thorax material, 55, 63

Gaufin, Arden R., 24, 37, 155, 162, 163
Gerhardt, Ken, 51
Gerken, Ted, 92–3
Giant Black Nature Nymph pattern,
    129–30
Golden Stone (Monty's), pattern, 147
Gold Ribbed Hare's Ear fly, 55
Green River, Wyoming, 104
Griffith, J. S., Jr., 18

Hair Wing Stonefly pattern, 143–4
Harden, Philip E., 30, 162
Harper, Peter P., 152, 163, 164
Harris, J. R., 100
hatch, *see* emergence
Hays, Richard A., 155
Henwing Bomber pattern, 143
hesitation/pause in line, 78, 81, 83, 84–5,
    92, 94, 96
Hesperoperla pacifica, 27, *illus.* 29
  adult (imitation), pattern, 137–8
  habitat, 137–8
  nymph: food and predation, 27–9;
    imitation, pattern, 137
Hewitt, Edward R., 86
Hexagenia limbata, hatch, 125, 143
Hildebrand, S. G., 163
Hilsenhoff, William L., 11, 153, 162
Hitchcock, Stephen W., 13, 161
Holt, Charles S., 164
hook
  Draper "Flat Bodied," 51
  for nymph (imitation), 44–5
Humphrey, William, 116
Hydroperla crosbyi, 33, *illus.* 34
Hynes, H. B. N., 13, 14, 27, 161, 164

Illies, J., 12, 161
imitation adult stonefly, *see* patterns for imitation adult stoneflies; stonefly adult, imitation
imitation nymph, *see* patterns for imitation nymphs; stonefly nymph, imitation
instar, 10
International Symposia on Plecoptera, 12
interrupted cast, 92, *illus.* 93
Inverted *Acroneuria* pattern, 63–4, *illus.* 63
Isoperla bilineata:
    adult (imitation), pattern, 143
    nymph, 33; imitation, patterns, 69–73, *illus.* 71–2, 138, 142
Isoperla fulva, 33–5
    adult (imitation), pattern, 146
    nymph (imitation), pattern, 146

Jewett, Stanley G., Jr., 162
Jones, D. S., 13, 164
Jorgensen, Poul, 43

Kaushik, N. K., 14, 164
Kerst, Cary D., 154, 162
Kim, Ke Chung, 163
Knight, A. W., 163
Kovalek, W. P., 163–4
Kreh, Lefty, 84, 88, 90
Krumholz, L. A., 31, 163
K's Butt Salmonfly, 107–108
    pattern, 109–16, *illus.* 109–14

latex
    as abdominal material, 53
    for nymph legs, artificial, 57
lead, melting, 49
leader, 84
    for "big waters," 91
    long, with long rod, 91
    for night fishing, 126
leaves, dead, importance to stoneflies, 13–14
legs of stonefly nymph, artificial, 57
Leuctridae, 22–3, *illus.* 23
    adult (imitation), pattern, 131–2, 134
life cycle of stonefly, 10

line, 79–81
    code letters, numbers, 80
    sink-tip type, 80, 91, 95
Little Black Stonefly Dry pattern, 135
Little Black Stonefly Nymph pattern, 131
Little Yellow Adult, with egg sac, pattern, 147

Madison River, Montana, 3–4, 94–5, 123–4
Magnin, Etienne, 152, 162
Malenka, behavioral drift patterns, 15, *illus.* 16
Martinez, Don, 54
Massachusetts, emergence dates in (table 1), 151
materials
    quill butts, 116
    for typing nymph flies, 44–58
    see also feathers; floss, woven; fur; latex; lead; monofilament; quill sheathing; rubber strands; Swannundaze; wire
Mathews, Craig, 129–30
mayfly
    Baetis, 17, 18
    nymph, distinguished from stonefly, 10
McClane, A. J., 54
McDiffett, W. F., 14, 164
McNeese, Dave, 32
    fly patterns, 132, 133, 134, 136–7, 144, 145, 146, 147
mending line, 81–3, illus. 81, 92
Mickel, Clarence E., 30, 162
Mickievicz, Jack, 56
Milam, Paul, 155
Miner, Michael, 155
molting, 10, *illus.* 101 (6–1); *see also* white nymph
monofilament:
    as abdominal material, 53
    removing "memory coils," 80
    on shooting-head line, 80
Mono Stonefly Nymph pattern, 139–40
Montana Stone pattern (for *P. californica*), 68–9
Montplaisir, R. "Monty"
    fishing techniques, 86–8
    Golden Stone pattern, 47
    wet-fly technique, 87–8, illus. 87
Monty's Golden Stone pattern, 147

motion of artificial flies, 43–4, 55
Mottled Stonefly Nymph pattern, 142
Müller, Karl, 14–15
Muttkowski, Richard, 37

Narf, Richard P., 153, 162
Neaviperla, 32
Nebeker, Alan V., 162
Needham, Paul R., 14, 164
Needlefly pattern, 134
Nemoura vallicularia, see *Soyedina vallicularia*
Nemouridae, 24–5
  adult (imitation), pattern, 131–2
Neoperla clymene, 29–30
  molting population, 102–103
Neve, Jay, and Don Fox, fly patterns, 131, 135, 140, 141–2, 143, 145–6
Neves, Richard J., 85, 151, 163, 164
Niemeyer, Ted, 43, 58
  fishing technique, 88–9, *illus.* 89
  on white nymph, 104
night fishing techniques, 124–6
North American Benthological Society (NABS), 12
nymph, *see* patterns for imitation nymphs; stonefly nymph, imitation; *also* nymph *under individual families, genera and species*
nymph, white, 99–105
  Alabaster Nymph, 104–105
  tying, 100, *illus.* 104
Nymphform (precut plastic), 50–1
Nymph Recognition Table, 40–1
nymph wing burner, *illus.* 56, 57

One-Feather Nymph pattern for *I. bilineata*, 70, 73, *illus.* 71
Orbendorfer, Reed Y., 163
Oregon, emergence dates in (table 4), 154
oval-shaped nymph, imitation, 46–7, *illus.* 47
ovipositing, 10–11

Paracapnia opis: adult (imitation), pattern, 135
Paragnetina immarginata, 27
Paragnetina media, 31–2, illus. 31
Paraleuctra occidentalis, 22

patterns for imitation adult stoneflies
  Brooks' Salmonfly, 121
  Calineuria californica, 137
  Hair Wing Stonefly, 143–4
  Henwing Bomber, 143
  Hesperoperla pacifica, 137–8
  Isoperla bilineata, 143
  Isoperla fulva, 146
  K's Butt Salmonfly, 109–16, *illus.* 109–14
  Little Black Stonefly Dry, 135
  Little Yellow, with egg sac, 147
  Needlefly, 134
  Polar Commander, 145–6
  Poly-Caddis Style Fly, 131–2
  Pteronarcys californica, 145
  Salmonfly, 117–21, *illus.* 118–20
  Taeniopteryx, 133
patterns for imitation nymphs
  Acroneuria, 58–63, *illus.* 60–2; Bill Simpson's, 64–8, *illus.* 65–8; Inverted, 63–4, *illus.* 63
  Black Woolly Bug 75, illus. 74
  Black Woolly Worm, 73–5, *illus.* 74
  Brooks' Montana Stone, 68–9
  Brown Woolly Worm, 74–5
  Calineuria californica, 136
  Catskill Curler, 138
  Claassenia, 130–1
  Curved *dorsata*, 140
  Curved *lycorias*, 141–2
  Delaware Yellow Stonefly Wet, 138
  Don's Brown Stonefly, 141
  Don's Mottled Stonefly, 142
  Early Brown Stonefly Wet, 133
  Giant Black Nature Nymph, 129–30
  Hesperoperla pacifica, 137
  Isoperla bilineata, 69–73
  Isoperla fulva, 146
  Little Black Stonefly, 131
  Mono Stonefly, 139–40
  Monty's Golden Stone, 147
  One-Feather Nymph, 70, 73, *illus.* 71–2
  Peltoperla, 135–6
  Pteronarcys californica, 144
  Red Brown Nymph, 134–5
  Taeniopteryx, 132
  Yellow Stonefly, 69–70
Patterson, M. F., 13, 164
pause/hesitation in line, 78, 81, 83, 84–5, 92, 94, 96
Pearson, W. D., 17
Peltoperla arcuata, 35

Peltoperla maria, 35–6, *illus.* 35
  food, 13
  habitat, 77
  nymph (imitation), pattern, 135–6
Peltoperlidae, 35–6
Penobscot River, west branch, Maine, 122
Perla (periodical), 12–13
Perlesta placida, 30–1
  eggs, 11
Perlidae, 27–32
  adult (imitation), pattern, 143–4
  habitat, 77
  nymph (imitation), patterns, 138
    139–40
Perlodidae, 33–5
  adult (imitation), pattern, 131–2
Phasganophora capitata, 27
  nymph (imitation), pattern, 147
Phillips, Robert W., 27, 164
Pirone, Dominick J., 14, 99
plastic nymph body (unweighted), 50–1,
    illus. 50
Plecoptera, *see* stonefly
pockets, fishing techniques for, 90–1
Polar Commander pattern, 145–6
pollution, 11
Poly-Caddis Style Fly pattern, 131–2
Pratt, John J., Jr., 100
Pteronarcella badia, 5, 36
Pteronarcella regularis, 36
Pteronarcyidae, 36–9
  adult (artificial), pattern, 143–4
  habitat, 77
  nymph (artificial), patterns, 138,
    139–40
Pteronarcys californica (salmonfly), 36–8
  adult, *illus.* 123; fishing for, 37–8,
    121–7; imitation, patterns, 109–16,
    illus. 109–14; 117–21, *illus.* 118–20;
    145
  hatch, 3–4, 38, 121–2
  nymph, *illus.* 37; and float fishing, 95;
    imitation, patterns, 68–9; 129–30;
    144 imitation, of quill, 52–3
Pteronarcys dorsata
  adult: drumming signals, 10; imitation,
    pattern, 145–6
  hatch, 122
  nymph, 5, 38–9, 140; imitation,
    patterns, 140; 141
Pteronarcys pictetti, 14, 38–9
Pteronarcys princeps, 38

Quammen, David, 130–1
quartering upstream cast, 127
Quebec, emergence dates in (table 2),
    152
quill butts, 116
quill sheathing
  as abdominal material, 52
  method of obtaining, 52–3, *illus.* 53
  and segmentation, 55

rainbow trout, food and predation,
    18–19
Red Brown Nymph pattern, 134–5
reel, 79
Reif, Ed, 122
Renzetti wing burner, *illus.* 56, 57
ribbing materials, 55
Richardson, Jay W., 37, 163
Ricker, William E., 12, 24, 155, 162
rod, 78–9
  for "big waters," 91
  for dry fishing, 123
  for float fishing, 95
  long, with long leader, 91
  for small streams, 127
Ross, Herbert H., 24, 162
rubber strands
  for legs of nymph, artificial, 57
  for tail of Bitch Creek nymph, 51–2
runs, fishing techniques for, 90–1

salmonfly, see *Pteronarcys californica*
Say, Thomas, 11
Schmookler, Paul, 6–7, 135–6
Schwiebert, Ernest, 26, 53
Scudder, G. E., 162
Seal-ex, 54
segmentation, materials for, 55
Sessions, Joann, 162
shooting-head line, 80–1, 93
Siegfried, C. A., 163
Simpson, Bill: *Acroneuria* pattern, 64–8,
    illus. 65–8
sinker, for weighting nymph, 49
sink-top line, 80, 91, 95
Snellen, Rosalyn K., 22–3, 30, 163
Soyedina vallicularia, 24–5
split-shot nymph, imitatation, 49–50,
    illus. 49
Stark, Bill P., 10, 161

steelhead, 140
Stewart, Kenneth W.
  on behavioral drift, 17
  bibliography, 161, 163, 164
  on Chloroperlidae nymphs, 32–3
  on drumming signals, 10
  on *I. fulva*, 33–4
  on molting nymphs, 102, 103
  on *P. californica*, 36
  on Perlidae nymphs, 28–30
  on Perlodidae nymphs, 33
  on pollution, 11
  on Taeniopterygidae nymphs, 25
  on *Z. claasseni*, 22–3
stonefly
  adult, *see* stonefly adult, imitation;
    also adult *under individual families,
    genera, and species*
  behavior and habits, 6, 11
  emergence dates, 6; tables, 151–7
  families, 21–39
  food, 13–14; bibliography, 163–4
  life cycle, 10
  life histories: bibliography, 163
  nymph, *see* stonefly nymph, imitation;
    also nymph *under individual
    families, genera, and species*
  research, 11–13
stonefly adult, imitation
  fishing for, 121–7
  patterns, *see* patterns for imitation
    adult stoneflies
  points to remember (list), 127
  tying, 107–21
stonefly nymph, imitation
  flat-bodied, 45–6, *illus.* 45
  flat oval-shaped, 48 and *illus.*
  materials for tying, 43–58, 100
  oval-shaped, 46–7, *illus.* 47
  patterns, *see* patterns for imitation
    nymphs
  split-shot, 49–50, *illus.* 49
  unweighted, 50–1, *illus.* 50
  weighting, 44–51
  white, 100
Strophopteryx fasciata, 26–7
  nymph (artificial), pattern, 133
Surdick, Rebecca F., 24, 163
Suwallia, 32, 33
Swannundaze, 52, 54, 55
Sweltsa, 32, 33
synthetics, as abdominal material, 54;
  see also latex

Systellognatha, 21–2, *illus.* 22, 27–39
Szcytko, Stanley W., 163

Taeniopterygidae, 25–7, *illus.* 25
  adult (imitation), patterns, 131–2, 133
  nymph (imitation), pattern, 132
Taeniopteryx nivalis, illus. 26, 27
tail of artificial nymph, 51–2
Tanaka, Hikaru, 14, 164
Tarter, D. C., 31, 163
thorax
  of fur, 63
  materials for, 55–7
Triznaka, 32, 33
trout: food and predation, 18–19
twitching method of casting, 124, 126
tying flies, *see* fly tying; patterns for
    imitation adult stoneflies; patterns
    for imitation nymphs

Un-Seal, 54
unweighted nymph, imitation, 50–1,
  illus. 50
upstream hold cast, 82, *illus.* 83, 124,
  127
U.S., western, emergence dates in (table
  5), 155–7

Vaught, George L., 29–30, 102, 163
Vinciguerra, Matt, 5
  fly patterns, 133, 138

Walton, Izaak, 54
Warr, Max, 108
water
  current, and casting, 82–3
  pollution, 11
  temperature, 11
Waters, Thomas F.
  on behavioral drift, 14–18 *passim*,
    85–6, 164
  on molting nymphs, 103
Watkins, W. C., 163
weighting imitation nymphs, 44–51
  flat-bodied, 45–6, *illus.* 45
  flat oval-shaped, 48 and *illus.*
  oval-shaped, 46–7, *illus.* 47
wet-fly fishing technique, 87–8, *illus.* 87

white nymph, 99–105
    Alabaster Nymph fly, 104–105
    tying, 100, *illus.* 104
Whitlock, Dave, 57, 83
Wigglesworth, Vincent, 100
wing case or pad, imitation, 56–7, *illus.*
    56
winter stoneflies, 6, 23–4
wire, lead fuse
    sizes, 45
    for weighting artificial nymphs, 45–8
    passim
Wisconsin, emergence dates in (table 3),
    153
wool, raw, as abdominal material, 54
Woolly Bear (Black Woolly Bug) pattern,
    75 and *illus.*

Woolly Worm, 54–5; *see also* Black
    Woolly Bug; Black Woolly Worm;
    Brown Woolly Worm
Wu, Chenfu Francis, 24–5, 163

Yamashito, Yaz, 43
Yellow Sallies, 32
    pattern, 131–2
Yellow Stonefly, pattern for *I. bilineata*,
    69–70, *illus.* 71–2
Yoraperla brevis, 35

Zapada haysi, 18
Zealeuctra claasseni, 22–3
Zwick, Peter, 12, 161

GRATEFUL ACKNOWLEDGMENT is made to the following for permission to use previously published material as sources for drawings and tables:

Figure 2–1 (Behavioral drift patterns for a *Malenka* species) is redrawn by permission from T. F. Waters, "Diel Patterns of Aquatic Invertebrate Drift in Northern Utah," *Utah Academy Proceedings,* Volume 46, page 42, 1969.

Figures 3–1 *(Taeniopteryx nivalis),* 3–3 (Nymphal wing pads), and 3–4 a & b (Tarsal segments, Taeniopterygidae and Nemouridae) redrawn by permission of Rebecca F. Surdick from *Stoneflies (Plecoptera) of Pennsylvania,* Bulletin 808, The Pennsylvania State University of Agriculture, 1976, by Rebecca F. Surdick and Ke Chung Kim.

Figure 3–2 *(Isogenus subvarians)* redrawn by permission of the State Geological and Natural History Survey of Connecticut from "The Plecoptera, or Stoneflies, of Connecticut" by Stephen W. Hitchcock.

Table 1 is adapted by permission of the New York Entomological Society from "Seasonal Succession and Diversity of Stoneflies (Plecoptera) in Factory Brook, Massachusetts," by Richard J. Neves, *Journal of the New York Entomological Society,* Volume 36, Number 3, 1978.

Table 2 is adapted by permission of Peter Harper from "Cycles Vitaux de Quelques Pléctoperes des Laurentides (Insectes)" by Peter Harper and Etienne Magnin, *Canadian Journal of Zoology,* Volume 47, Number 4, 1969.

Table 3 is adapted by permission of the Great Lakes Entomological Society from "Emergence Pattern of Stoneflies (Plecoptera) in Otter Creek, Wisconsin," by Richard P. Narf and William L. Hilsenhoff, *The Great Lakes Entomologist,* Volume 7, Number 4, 1974.

Table 4 is adapted by permission of Blackwell Scientific Publications Ltd., Oxford, England, from "Emergence Patterns of Plecoptera in a Stream in Oregon, U.S.A.," by Cary D. Kerst and N. H. Anderson, *Freshwater Biology,* Volume 4, 1974.

Table 5 is adapted by permission of the American Entomological Society from "The Stoneflies (Plecoptera) of Montana" by Arden R. Gaufin, William E. Ricker, Michael Miner, Paul Milam, and Richard A. Hays, *Transactions of the American Entomological Society,* Volume 98, 1972.

A Note About the Authors

Eric Leiser, a master fly tyer, teacher, and expert on the materials of the craft, is the author of *The Complete Book of Fly Tying* and *Fly-Tying Materials* and co-author (with Larry Solomon) of *The Caddis and the Angler.* He is president of The Rivergate, a fly fisherman's supply house, and is on the board of United Fly Tyers and an active member of Theodore Gordon Fly Fishers, the Federation of Fly Fishermen, and Trout Unlimited. He lives in Wappingers Falls, New York.

Robert H. Boyle, a senior writer for *Sports Illustrated,* is the author of *The Hudson River, A Natural and Unnatural History* and *Bass* (with photographs by Elgin Ciampi) and co-edited The Fly-Tyer's Almanac series. An active conservationist, he is president of the Hudson River Fishermen's Association and received the Salmo Award from the Theodore Gordon Fly Fishers in 1964 and the Outdoor Life Conservation Award in 1976. He lives in Cold Spring, New York.

A NOTE ON THE TYPE

The text of this book was set by computer-driven cathode-ray
tube in Century Schoolbook, a typeface based on Century
Expanded, which was designed in 1894 by Linn Boyd Benton
(1844–1932). Benton cut Century Expanded in response to
Theodore De Vinne's request for an attractive, easy-to-read
typeface to fit the narrow columns of his *Century Magazine*.
Early in the nineteen hundreds Morris Fuller Benton
updated and improved Century in several versions for his
father's American Type Founders Company. Century remains
the only American typeface cut before 1910 still widely used
today.

Composed by The Haddon Craftsmen, Scranton, Pennsylvania
Printed and bound by Halliday Lithogroph, West Hanover,
Massachusetts